CW00525178

Born six weeks early, during the War years, life never got any easier. This lead to a biography of his birth and early years and was documented in a booklet called "The Life and Times of Eddie Smith", published by Anne Bradford of "Hunt End Books". This true account of his life follows on from where, at the age of 16, he joined HM Forces, at which point a series of events—unintended and mostly humorous—gave the impression that he could be a security risk.

## Dedication

To my long suffering wife of 40 years, Gail; my children, Jamie and Corrina; and my grandchildren, Sam and Ellie.

Eddie Smith

# A PERFORATION

## ON THE TOILET ROLL OF LIFE

AUSTIN MACAULEY PUBLISHERS™

LONDON • CAMBRIDGE • NEW YORK • SHARJAH

A CIP catalogue record for this title is available from the British Library.

ISBN 9781788484909 (Paperback)
ISBN 9781788484916 (Hardback)
ISBN 9781788484923 (E-Book)

www.austinmacauley.com

First Published (2018)
Austin Macauley Publishers Ltd™
25 Canada Square
Canary Wharf
London
E14 5LQ

# Acknowledgements

To my oldest friend and author, Trevor Dalton, whose
encouragement made this possible.

# Chapter 1
## Enlisting

It was a cold September morning the day I left home to join the Army as a boy soldier. I had always wanted to join the navy, but here I was, beginning a journey that was to start me off on an army apprenticeship. I have often wondered why I should have suddenly decided to choose to be a soldier rather than a sailor.

A short booklet was written about my earlier life, which was a bit controversial, and in it I mention the fact that I was a vehicle apprentice, and well thought of.

In fact, every time I indicated that I might change my vocation, they upped my wages. I knew it would hurt my employers if I found work elsewhere. Joining the forces seemed an easy way out, in which they wouldn't be upset.

I was to spend the next three years at the Army Apprenticeship School at Arborfield in Berkshire.

The first morning in junior company at Arborfield Berkshire was certainly a shock to the system; from reveille at 6 am, the rest of the day seemed to consist of nothing but screaming, swearing and shouting orders.

This continued until 9 pm, we then showered and got into bed for last post at 10 pm.

We obviously despised the reveille bugle each morning, but loved the last post at night—signifying a well-earned respite from our demanding daily regime.

The process we went through had to be tough to take us all to our respective breaking points—to weed out the mentally and physically weak amongst us, in order to prepare us for what lay ahead in the three years of training that lay before us. The physically and mentally draining daily routine went on for three months non-stop. It was harsh but not brutal; that was to come when we moved down into the companies.

Junior company was housed in one block at the top end of a very large parade square. We were segregated from the rest of the school, and didn't know it then but it was for our own safety.

The four companies (A, B, C and D) were in what were known as spider blocks—two either side of the large square. From an aerial view, spider block would resemble two capital E's back to back, joined by two shower blocks in between.

At the bottom end of the square was the canteen (mess hall) with four large long rectangular billets either side, which housed senior company—boys who had turned into men, having survived their three years, and due to leave to be posted into the regular Army after passing out of boys' school.

My big, big, big mistake was that I didn't get the concept of 'jipping', none of us did, but I was to find out the hard way, and every one of my peers learnt from it.

The three years are split into nine divisions. Starting with junior company (division 1) up to senior company (division 9). Nine were superior to eight, eight to seven and so on, all the way down to junior company. The system meant that you were literally a slave, or as in Eton, a fag to those in divisions above you, especially if you were in any sort of queue. It was a 'pecking order' in the true sense.

Any division above you had the right to push in front, which they did continuously.

The first time I experienced this queue jumping was while I was waiting in line for dinner, and at this point I was not aware of the 'superiority rule' that other divisions had come to accept

I ended up getting into a confrontation with boys from mixed divisions all at once, who themselves had been pushed back down the line.

Backing down from an altercation was not something I ever did because of my stubborn nature. I understood, which was stupid in the circumstances. Their threats rang out loud and clear! I was shocked at the resentment it had caused and the promise of retribution which I would have to endure on my leaving junior company.

If I had known at that time that they most definitely meant what they were threatening, I would probably have left the school there and then.

When we were all transferred down to the companies, it was the night before the school broke up for a four-week holiday over Easter.

That night when we arrived down in the spider block of D company, I realised how much trouble I was in.

There were about 20 to 30 lined up in single file, all in priority of divisional status, waiting in turn to have a go at me. From that day to this, I have never known what total fear was.

After I had stored my kit away and my shaking became uncontrollable, I realised I might as well go out and face my tormentors, even if it meant the biggest kicking of my life.

I was close to tears, not because of the fear of being hurt, but more for the reason that so many people could hate me with such passion all at once, and all in the same place. It seemed inconceivable.

A good majority of my peers in our billet were determined to go out with me as a show of force. All eight of them.

I crept out of the barrack room under a pretence of some excuse or other, which made me feel like some sort of hero, like they do in the movies. It certainly made me feel better trying to protect my comrades.

When I left the barrack room, I could hear the voices of my tormentors around the next corner of the corridor. My heart was thumping so loud I thought it would explode. As soon as the lined-up mob saw me, the heckling and abuse started, but within seconds it all went deathly quiet.

Unknown to me, my junior sergeant and his corporal had arrived on the scene, and had followed me down the corridor. They were to be our mentors, and more importantly our protectors, after the Easter break.

The mob went silent and dispersed after being threatened by the two heroes. I didn't know it at the time, but it was out of a mixture of respect and fear of them.

They both were successful boxers in the school team, and I believe one, if not both, went on a couple of years later to represent England at the Olympics.

# Chapter 2
## The Companies

They protected me as they thought that I was a potential candidate to join their boxing team, and that I showed courage and bravery; if they only knew.

Anyway, I realised that to be protected in the coming months I had to join the boxing squad.

I always remember that my fighting weight was the same as Muhammad Ali (Cassius Clay) when he started his pro career, difference being that Clay was six foot three and I was only five foot seven.

For those long six months before the Sergeant and Corporal left Arborfield I took a lot of beatings in the ring, because boxing as a heavyweight I was up against six footers. I hardly landed a punch. And was I glad to finally step down. I had no further trouble from the mob, except for one. There has to be one, doesn't there.

A few months later, four of us in our barrack room chipped in £5 each and bought a car: a 1938 Wolsey from a young lieutenant. I was the only one with a licence, therefore the designated driver. That first weekend a group of six of us went tenpin bowling in Reading. Unfortunately, I mounted a high kerb on a sharp corner,

These cars were built like tanks in those days, no wonder gangsters in America used to favour them. Apparently, it seemed like there was no damage, so we made it back to camp before curfew.

The next day, the same group of us, plus another big heavy car, a V8 Pilot with another half a dozen mates on board, went into the countryside for a drink.

A big attraction was the 'Little Chef' caravan on the A30. Supposedly the first Little Chef in Britain. Most of us were hooked on their ham'n egg Sandwiches.

On the way back, driving along a country road, there was an almighty explosion and the cowling covering the engine flapped up for a split second like two angel's wings.

We pulled over and got out. The first thing we noticed was the oil behind us on the road. We looked underneath and spotted a hole in the engine sump. Realisation then sank in, and we were aware that the hole must have occurred when I mounted the kerb the night before.

The V8 was such a powerful car that it towed us all back to the Apprentice College, where we had permission to put the car in the engineering workshop, and were told we could work on repairing the damage in our own time.

This is where the big twist comes into the story.

When we removed the engine sump, we found that the actual piston head had completely disintegrated into hundreds of small pieces, which was unusual, but not as startling as finding the piston conrod in the sump all twisted.

We realised that this couldn't be, as conrods were constructed from cast iron and would be impossible to twist; they would snap first.

If we were surprised at that, what came next shocked us more. Whilst a group of us were getting the engine out, one of my peers decided to clean the parts in petrol in a bowl on the bench. He startled us with shouts of 'come look at this'.

We went over to see what was making him excitable, and there all clean and wrapped up in a cloth was the conrod, with a bigger twist in than we had noticed before, but also plain to see was an embossed swastika.

None of us could believe that such a thing could happen in a car which was the pride of Britain in its day.

Even the Instructors and teachers had no explanation. They asked if the school could keep the item and exhibit it in a glass case for all to see. Which they did.

The story doesn't end there, as over the years I've told the tale of our find many times.

Twenty years later, working as a rep, I related the find to a store man at 'Smiths Electricals' in Walsall.

13

He immediately said, "Did you buy the car in the '60s?"

I said, "Yes."

"Was it bought from a young officer?"

Again I said, "Yes."

He said, "Well, there's your explanation."

His logical assessment would have done Hercule Poirot proud. It went like this.

After the war, only high ranking officers were allowed to take their cars to occupied Germany. It was almost impossible to obtain any type of car spares in Europe, with the exception of Volkswagen, the people's car, which Hitler had instigated. These were likely to have swastika embossed parts somewhere on them.

The Germans being such highly skilled engineers probably had the know-how to re-temper cast iron, to enable to twist the conrod to fit the specifications of a foreign car.

This high ranking officer probably had children in England. If he had a son, the chances are that he would likely be sent to a private, pre-Army School, such as the Duke of York, which is similar to Eton.

He then would have passed his car on to his son when he was of age. That theory would fit all the timelines.

Forces personnel are well-known for collecting memorabilia: beer mats, football cards, beer glasses and such like. I wanted to be original, so I never bothered. Until, on one of our nights out in Reading, I happened to need the toilet.

In those days the majority of WC's had a chain flush, but when I flushed the system the chain came away in my hand. It was very decorative, in a Victorian style. That started me off, but I kept it a secret in case any of my peers copied me, and there is a finite supply.

All went well until a good many months later, when it was reported in the local papers that the police were hot on the trail of the vandals targeting toilets in the area.

I panicked and, that night, went out and buried my substantial collection of chains on the outskirts of the football ground. I always wondered if they were ever found.

One early incident which sticks out as very funny happened on our first visit to a Chinese Restaurant in Reading. They were quite a new concept in the '60s.

Anyway, on one of our many boozed up weekends, one of my peers, Jock, who liked the thought of mastering different languages, but loved to communicate when he could, insisted on ordering the meals for the six of us by using his brand of self-taught sign language,

In those days, it was rare if any of the waiters could speak English, which never really mattered, as all the food and drinks were numbered.

Jock really tried hard and was annoyed if anyone tried to help him. The waiter left our table looking as though he understood; he even repeated what Jock said in his Mandarin dialect: six 123s to start. What could go wrong? All the beer numbers were in the hundreds and 123 was bitter.

We sat and waited for a while, looking forward to our first drink of the evening. When the kitchen door swung open, not one but three Chinese waiters all came out at once, each one carrying bowls of soup.

Soup was listed with single digit numbers: one, two, three and so on. Jock had inadvertently ordered each of us three different types of soup.

In our barrack room there were 12 of us, and like all teenagers, living, eating and playing in such a relatively small space there were many arguments, but the brotherly bond that was formed was something special.

The one person who I felt especially close to was a Scot from Ayrshire called Jamie (Jock) Black, a great practical joker and a natural comedian.

I had always been very gullible, even now, but in those days I was as green as they come.

He convinced me that Haggis, which in Scotland are called Gomeronches, all have two legs, one leg shorter than the other. This enables them to run around mountains easier and faster. I actually believed him.

My closest friend was Norman Swan (Swanee), who but for his eyesight would be a pilot.

Another person I felt especially close to was Rob Watts; he excelled at sports, especially running events. Bob's closest mate in our room was a shy retiring type called Billy, who was very into music and played an instrument; he was a past scholar from the Duke of York's, which probably meant his family were heavily connected with the forces.

At this point, I have to mention a Basil Riggs (not his real name). We were very close and he would confide in me on very personal matters, but at best most of our peers would only tolerate him because of the outlandish tales he would tell, as they would choose not to believe him.

I remember that after a long seven-week holiday in the summer, on our return, we would all reiterate what we had been doing during the holidays. Nothing really special, just normal teenager stuff, but Basil always went one better. Such as, his father had paid for a course of flying lessons in a helicopter, and he was close to getting his licence. Each week it seemed something extraordinary had taken place in his life.

One day, he told me he had been given special permission to confide a great secret to me, but the proviso was that I had to go to London with him that weekend.

I had only been to the capital once before as a young boy, so I was excited about it, especially as it was all free, Basil always had plenty of money.

On that weekend, we arrived in London and went to a pub in Soho and Baz brought the drinks over.

He then swore me to secrecy and told me the following.

His father was a major in the Intelligence Services during the war, and was one of the first to go into the bunker where Hitler met his end.

In the rooms, which were occupied by Hitler's second in command, Martin Bormann, a baby was found (Baz). The Major brought the child back and he and his wife formally adopted him. I thought *here we go again*, but Baz got up and said, "I'm relieved now I've told someone, but please wait here in the pub, while I go out and find why I have been summoned to London this weekend."

Off he went and left me, I was surprised how quick he had been. He came in looking all ashen and bought two more pints, came and sat down, took a deep breath and pulled a gun furtively out of his jacket to show me. He then informed me that he may be in danger. To help alleviate any chance of him being recognised, all the pictures of Martin Bormann had been removed from all of the relevant books back in the school library. I checked and they all had.

I kept asking myself, "Is he telling me this because I'm that gullible?"

When we reached 7th division in 1963, six of us decided to book the forthcoming summer holiday together. There were only two viable choices of resorts for fun loving, highly charged testosterone teenagers to contemplate going to: Lloret de Mar or Lido de Jesolo.

After days of soul searching, we agreed on Lloret.

Lloret was nothing like the bustling, vibrant resort that it is now; it was in its transitional stage from small fishing village to a lively party resort.

We couldn't all get into the same hotel, there wasn't much choice in those days, there were only about three large hotels, which meant that we were split into pairs in three different locations.

Swanee and myself drew the short straw and found ourselves in an annexe of our hotel, located up a side street; but we had our meals at the main hotel.

In those days, tourists were warned not to drink the water, and bottled water was virtually unheard of. Spanish brandy was dirt cheap, so we bought a bottle just to clean our teeth with.

One particularly heavy drinking night, we parted but made arrangements to meet on the beach the next morning at a certain time.

I was late in getting up, but I couldn't awaken Swanee, so I wrote a quick note as to where we might be later. Just as I was leaving, and about to light a cigarette, I realised it was our last match.

I had a cunning plan. There were plenty of candles about the room, as in those days blackouts at night were common place: every shop, eating establishment and bar had candles close at hand. It would be the norm for the lights to go out at least half a dozen times a night.

So I lit a candle and put it on the bedside dresser, propped up against the Brandy bottle, so at least when Swanee woke up, he could have a ciggy.

Off I went to the beach in search of the other four. When I found them, it was only a matter of minutes before Swanee turned up, looking really stressed out. He was normally the calm one of our group. He explained what had happened. It was an explosion that had woken him, oh, and also the flames lapping the bedside table that really caught his attention.

I learnt my lesson and have never propped up a candle against a spirit bottle since.

In those days Franco was in power, and one had to be careful not to fall foul of the law.

It's hard to believe that it was forbidden to hold hands in the street, even if you were with the wife. It was allowed to have only the top button of a shirt undone while you were off the beach. Police were non-existent, but the black capped Militia were everywhere.

Electric storms would knock the lights out throughout the resort at least half a dozen times a night. What made the situation bizarre was the fact that it seemed every shop and bar would restart their music all at the same moment. The only trouble was that it was nearly always the same LP: Please, Please, Me, by the Beatles. There were not that many disco's or music bars compared to nowadays, the main ones being the Brazilia Club in the Carrer del Rector, The Cavern carved out of the hillside, and most importantly of all, the Western Saloon in the Carrera sta Cristina.

I say importantly because the Western Saloon was probably the most vibrant, and heart and soul of the resort.

The Militia would shut it down every two weeks. Why? It was because the sitting Mayor looked on singing as decadent, especially if the song *If I Had a Hammer* by *Trini Lopez* was played.

It's still there now, only that all the doors and windows have been bricked up for decades. I believe it is now a Yates's pub.

Anyway, one night I was so drunk that I could not stand, let alone walk. I was a bit of a let down to my comrades who were on the pull, and with me in tow their chances were diminished.

At that moment two Manchester blokes from our hotel happened to be passing. They assessed the situation and volunteered to take me back to the hotel, thus unburdening my mates.

Now these two Northerners were a great laugh, and were the type who could pull any bird they wanted. They had looks and charisma by the bucketful. Problem was they were openly Gay. This worried me a lot.

In my drunken state, I immediately started panicking; they were well over six foot and had muscles on top of muscles. They found no trouble in carrying me, even though I put up the best struggle that I could in my semi-conscious state.

Half way back to the hotel, there were three young men approaching us on their way down the hill for a night out. What made these three really stand out was their dress sense. They were wearing three piece suits and ties, which made them stick out like sore thumbs.

I seized my chance to escape, and started screaming that they were poufs, and trying to drag me back to have their wicked way with me. I sensed that they didn't want to get involved, so as they drew level with us, I lunged at the nearest one, grabbing hold of his jacket and begged them to help me. I felt the worst as most of his buttons shot off his jacket.

Anyway, it didn't seem to bother them, and a discussion took place between all five of them.

Two of my would-be rescuers had very strong scouse accents and after a very short discussion, it was decided that I should go with the Liverpudlians. So off we went back down to the bright lights of Lloret.

They looked familiar, and I was sure that they could be famous.

They took me to the Brazilia Club, and as we approached the door, they told me if I couldn't sober up enough to walk unaided into the club then they would leave me outside to fend for myself.

It took all the willpower I could muster, but I did it. They sat me at a table in a corner, at the back of the club and put a drink in front of me. I knew I couldn't even manage a sip; I was still unable to string a sentence together, so they just ignored me. I remember feeling safe and happy though.

I have no idea how long I sat there, but a time came when the Spanish group took a break, left their equipment, and exited the club, I suppose for a breath of fresh air, or a fag.

As soon as they did, my newly found companions got up from our table, walked through the tables and crowds and on to the stage. They picked up the Spanish groups instruments and started playing. The crowd went wild, as if they knew who they were. I remember thinking how brilliant the music was, but after a short time all hell broke loose. The Militia came storming into the club, blowing whistles and waving their Tommy guns around.

The club emptied in seconds. I don't know what happened after that, or how I got back, or what happened to the Liverpool lads. I always wondered who they were.

# Chapter 3
## Osnabruck 1964–1966

On completing my three year apprenticeship, and leaving the REME College at Arborfield, my first posting was to Osnabruck, Germany.

I was always a shy, timid, introverted sort of person, with a deep love for the Army, but this posting soon turned me into a rebel, and amongst other things, led me to sending a declaration of war to the Ministry of Defence, with copies of my declaration sent to four of the major newspapers of the day. This was the start of a four-year long rebellion against the Army.

By the end of my Army career, I had turned from an obedient, loyal soldier into a Sgt Bilko type figure.

I was the arch typical case, a victim of circumstance, being in the wrong place at the wrong time.

There were two main characters initially involved in these unfortunate incidents, ('Mad' Major Lawless and Captain Fielding,) who, years later, both returned to my life and had major impacts.

The start of my career nosedive happened almost immediately after leaving the Apprentice College, actually, the first week.

I had passed my exams as a Vehicle Electrician working on 12 volt and 24 volt systems. My first job was to sort out a very large 380 volt A/C industrial machine.

*I can do that*, I thought, kidding myself.

I was aided by one of my peers, Max, who like me had just left college. He had trained as a mechanic.

*No probs*, I thought.

Max was very keen. Too keen! He jumped straight in without thinking of the danger associated with high voltage electricity. He argued that all was safe, as we had took out the fuses, but I was sure that this very large industrial machine was still live.

After what seemed like a lifetime of arguing, he still wouldn't listen.

So in my frustration, I did what had become natural when working on low voltage systems, which was to short the cable to earth as I had done thousands of times on vehicles to see if there is a spark.

I did this with my heavy duty wooden handled screwdriver.

It wasn't so much a spark as an explosion! As well as the burning sensation on my hand caused from the screwdriver melting, we both stood there for a lifetime; frightened to move, we had both been temporarily blinded.

I felt vindicated that I was right.

The CO never saw it that way when I was marched in front of him. This was the first of many 'small chats' we were to have.

I remember him saying that the combined allied air forces couldn't knock out this German workshop during the period of the war, but I had managed it in one week. The CO was forced to call in the Royal Engineers to dig up the roads to repair the cables beneath.

That set the seal on the relationship between the Major and myself for the remainder of my time there

It should be said that I wasn't the only one of my comrades from Arborfield that had the occasional mishap.

I remember Baz being given a job to do on a ten ton truck. On the job card all it stipulated was an electrical fault. He started up the truck, and everything seemed to be working all right so he switched off the ignition and looked for someone to give him more details about the fault.

That's when everything turned sour. The engine carried on running. *Ah*, he thought, *that must be the fault.*

He methodically started disconnecting each wire in the dashboard that he logically thought was causing the problem, but still the engine wouldn't stop running. So he tossed reason to one side, and began to strip all wires out of the cab, starting

22

with all the connections on the light switch, the heaters, and the interior light. He even went under the truck like a person obsessed and disengaged the brake lights

Eventually, the Staff Sergeant in charge of the work time sheets came along to find out what was taking Baz so long because the job should have been finished hours ago.

When Baz had calmed down, the NCO opened the door of the cab and said "look", and put his hand on the accelerator pedal, and pulled it backwards. "That's how you stop a diesel engine from running!" he barked.

When he saw the mess of wires, hanging dashboard, and dismantled gauges on the inside, they towed the truck outside to be repaired at a future date.

Another one of our comrades took a whole day trying to find out what was causing a ticking noise in an engine. The faster that the engine revved, the faster the noise was. This turned out to be a broken radiator grill, which was catching the fan. There were lots of happenings involving our intake, so it wasn't only me getting into trouble.

At this stage I should point out how and why the Major was given the prefix 'Mad'.

He had little quirks, such as on monthly inspections he would crawl under lorries with his white nylon gloves on, in search of dirt.

The first Winter Admin inspection, which is conducted by very high ranking officers, showed this up in a massive way.

It was a very cold November and the night before the inspection. He had all ranks, including officers, out at night sweeping up all the dirt and mud that the tanks and halftrack vehicles had left on the roads. We all worked until nearly midnight. The tools which we used were spades and brushes along with high pressure water hoses.

After the big freeze of that night all of the roads in the workshop sector had been turned into a giant ice rink.

The next morning everyone was slipping and sliding to get on parade and into position, but we shouldn't have worried as the Admin Inspection Team was also slipping.

The worst oddball quirk of all was his strictly enforced order that headgear must be worn at all times with no exceptions. It was an impractical rule, which everyone broke whilst working on vehicles, especially as many times you might be working upside down.

Both of these rules were to impact on me some months later, big time, but they were nothing compared to what was coming next.

Our large workshop was in a compound shared with the Queen's Own Highlanders Regiment, and they were responsible for the security of the area, with armed soldiers patrolling the camp both inside and out.

We looked after our own workshop area within this zone, but we were only armed with pickaxes. This is probably why none of us took guard duty that seriously. The pickaxes were never loaded.

The next incident was talked about for years to come, and eventually became folklore.

Inside our REME sector we had our own club, where almost everyone on patrol duty popped in and spent a couple of hours each night having the odd drink, instead of walking the inside perimeter and checking the wide variety of vehicles outside the workshop.

I was no exception, and on this cold December night I probably stayed longer than usual.

Before my spell of patrolling was over I left the club to return to the Guard house a good half hour early, which was the norm, as most of us had a hot drink before we got into our sleeping bags.

My mate Rob Watts was due on next; he was a keep fit fanatic and it never bothered him that the club would probably be shut, but at least my coming back early gave him the option to go for a drink.

I started to undress and get into my sleeping bag, when the Corporal of the guard came running in, seeming very agitated. The officer in charge that night was a raw recruit straight out of Sandhurst, and was known to be keen.

What was causing concern was the fact that it had started snowing heavily, and everyone knew that this young green officer would circle the perimeter to check on footprints.

My mate Rob had volunteered to go out early and use it as a training run, and put as many footprints on the ground as possible.

*Great*, I thought, and soon was tucked up for the night and in the land of nod.

I don't know how long I was asleep, but I was rudely awakened, being prodded with a baton with which officers are equipped.

The fresh faced Lieutenant looked angry and said, "Smith you were the last on duty, get dressed and meet me outside!"

Once outside, the interrogation started on whether or not I had been drinking.

Of course I denied it.

We started off trudging through the snow. He kept on quizzing me on the serious offence of drinking on duty as we trudged along. I was relieved to see that Bob had done me proud with the amount of footsteps he had planted. *I owe him big time,* I thought.

Still the lecture of drinking on duty continued, and I repeatedly denied it.

Finally we reached the main workshop compound, where all the finished and waiting to be worked on vehicles were parked. They were strewn about facing in all directions, covered with a blanket of snow.

Then I saw the problem I faced, and the reason the young officer kept on probing.

Now my stature I would kindly describe as portly and athletically challenged. Rob, in his enthusiasm, had run around the exterior, and had jumped up and over every vehicle parked in the compound: jeeps, 3 tonner's, 10 tonner's, half tracks and even the tanks. All I could say was that I wanted to keep warm. Without proof, I suppose he had to accept my explanation.

I'm sure it would have been a topic in the Officers Mess. If it was, it would be another reason for the Major to take me off his Christmas card list

The next minor incident which caused the Major to have words with me was a few months after the Winter break.

There was a monthly inspection due, but this time I had a cunning plan on how to have my vehicle, which was a 7 ton Bedford truck, dust free and ready for when the CO and his little white nylon gloves did their inspection

Most people would get up exceptionally early on the morning of the inspection, and give it one last dusting, having painted their vehicles a few days before.

My plan was, now that I held the keys to the Electrical store and workshop, that I would leave off painting my truck until the very last moment, i.e. the day before, and leave it in its allotted parking space between the rest of the vehicles to dry overnight.

I didn't know it was going to rain did I?

When the Major and his team turned up for the inspection the next morning, he stood there with his mouth open, looking past all of us on Parade, eyes fixed only on the Vehicle Park.

It was only when we were dismissed and told to stand by our vehicles that I realised it was my truck causing his consternation. My Bedford stuck out like a Bishop in a brothel, as it was several shades lighter than the regulation Army green. He wasn't well pleased, and ordered me to repaint it within the next 48 hours.

The next incident, although relatively small, must have caused him considerable embarrassment. We were on a Military exercise, travelling through dense forest in the middle of the night. The objective of the exercise was to move the Brigade undetected from point A to B. Can you imagine how disorientating it is with no lights on, not even knowing uphill from downhill? The long convoy had come to a standstill. It was total silence.

Then someone shouted that the ten ton truck in front was backing into us. I looked up and realised that the space between us was quickly diminishing, so I immediately hit the horn, and we were all shouting warnings to the driver of the truck, but the crunch came seconds later. It was only when we had exited the vehicle that we realised that we were confused by the total darkness, and it was *my* jeep that had been moving, and had collided into the back truck. Oops.

It was at about this time that two major events took place, which were to change my life and set my future on a different course for the rest of my Army career and beyond.

My father was disabled due to a massive stroke which had occurred a few years before. In fact, the Doctors said at that time that they never expected him to live past the weekend, but he was made of sterner stuff than most.

He seemed all but cured, except for a pronounced limp, and had a special spring on the toecap of his shoes to help lift his foot off the floor.

He more than encouraged me to enlist as a boy soldier, and I hardly gave his state of heath any thought, as we had lived with his condition for a long time. (All this was covered by author Anne Bradford's booklet about my early life, entitled *The Life and Times of Eddie Smith*.)

I was informed by the second in command, a Captain Fielding, that the Major wanted to see me urgently.

I was marched into his office, and within two minutes I was back outside trying to digest what he had briefly told me. My father had suffered another major stroke, and was not expected to live for more than 48 hours.

My travel documents had been prepared, and I was flying from Gutersloh airport later that day on two weeks compassionate leave.

Captain Fielding showed me a lot of compassion, but said he had to inform me of something, which wouldn't be generally told to those it concerned until the next day, and he made me promise not to tell my peers if I should see them in the next hour or two before leaving for my flight.

This other bombshell, which was only specific to Jock, Baz and myself, was the aftermath of a Ministry of Defence statement given to all apprentices at Arborfield halfway through our three year training.

The M.O.D had decided that all electricians in REME would be made redundant at a near future date. All three of us had been enrolled on an Airframe and Engines course to be held at a later date.

I was given a list of alternative courses to look at, but the Army would never sanction a course which would down grade an individual.

Can you imagine how it felt, having been informed 18 months into a three year apprenticeship that once we had passed our trade exams we would be made redundant.

Time passed, and we all tried to forget about this axe hanging over our heads.

So I took the flight home with a heavy heart. Worrying about my future wasn't an issue; just worrying about my father's health and especially what my mother was going through was utmost in my mind.

As before, my father was much more durable than the medical profession had reckoned, and at the end of my two weeks' leave, he was partly mobile His speech was very badly affected, but he was able to take the dog for a walk. I had been able to really help him to get about, but my mother was very small and frail and into her '70s, and she found it a struggle coping with the physical side that was needed in the care of my father.

I returned to Osnabruck, but had only been back about 10 days when the Major called me back into his office, for the same two minute chat, and off I was again on another two week compassionate leave.

I really have no idea just how many compassionate leaves I had in a six month period, but this second one had a profound effect on my future.

I realised that it was expected of me to end my Army career and look after Dad. It was noticeable that at the end of my home leaves, his improvement was always remarkable.

My adopted mother, at the age of 72, decided to give up work, so that she could be there to look after my father's daily needs.

Mother was one of twenty-one siblings, and my father one of nine, and they weren't shy at putting their oars in, and telling me what was expected of me.

I must admit that it was with great sadness that I wrote out my application, and applied for a compassionate discharge from the forces. Even with all of my mishaps I truly loved being in the Army.

In between my absences another couple of incidents occurred, one of which definitely made me rethink my future.

The next incident ended up in my facing a lengthy interrogation by the SIB (Special Investigation Branch).

One hot July day, I was hanging upside down working on a ten ton truck, and I happened to glance across the wasteland towards the Guard Room, which was between me and the truck on which I was working.

What caught my eye was what looked like smoke around the parked Land Rover at the rear of the Guard Room. It was such a hot day that I put it down to my imagination or heat haze. On my second look, it definitely was smoke billowing around the vehicle, and it was either on fire or about to catch fire.

I leapt into action and grabbed the fire extinguisher from under the seat of the truck, and raced across the wasteland shouting "Fire! Fire! Fire!" at the top of my voice.

Halfway there, I realised that I was breaking the Major's cardinal sin. As usual I was not wearing my Beret. I panicked big time, and headed back to get my headdress.

My shouts of fire had brought people out of the workshops and surrounding buildings, only to see a Jeep on fire and me running away from it.

Oops.

The Major didn't bother finding out the whys and wherefores, but had me arrested and held on open arrest until the SIB arrived.

I was held overnight, and the investigation took the best part of the next day. I got the distinct impression that they thought it was funny. I suppose all the witness accounts backed me up, but I think that they felt that their callout had been unnecessary. I don't remember the headgear rule being enforced so rigidly from then on.

Even I had some sympathy for the Major after the next episode, which I am sure caused him a degree of embarrassment. Again, not entirely my fault, and it could have happened to anyone.

The Brigade was on a large NATO exercise in the Hertz Mountains.

The objective of this war game was for us, the REME, to act the part of terrorists, and to find the Infantry Regiments who had to make their way from Point A to Point B.

After our illustrious leaders had figured out which route the enemy was going to take, all we had to do was lie in wait for them to come our way and engage them. Sounded easy enough

Again I will say it really is disorientating being in a forest in the dead of night, with no lights whatsoever, not even the moon.

Captain Fielding came into our six man tent at about 9.30 at night and told us that we were all on guard duty starting at ten o'clock. Each one doing a two hour shift.

"We will start with you, Smith. Go down to the end of the track, at the north end of camp, and relieve Stuart of his guard duty. Wilson, who is with him, will be relieved an hour later. If you hear any unusual noise, which you attribute to vehicles or men, then report back as quickly and quietly as you can."

It was a dry warm night, what could possibly go wrong?

I proceeded down the track after finally finding out what he meant by the North side of camp.

I trod cautiously and quietly at first, bumping into the occasional tree; then I thought to myself, *if I go this quietly then I might pass them without being seen.* So I thought I would sing, but not too loudly. Just loud enough for somebody hiding in the undergrowth to hear me, and then challenge me. I needed a song that I knew the words to.

The first song to pop into my head was 'Three Wheels on My Wagon' by the New Christy Minstrels. After repeating the song for the umpteenth time, and each time singing it louder and louder, I realised that the end of this track seemed to go on forever, and I was sure I must have passed them, or that I was on the wrong track.

I had just made up my mind to turn back, when I saw a light through the forest, so I reasoned that it must be them. So off I trudged down the track, walking more briskly as the trees didn't seem so dense.

I couldn't believe how long it took me, but the light was getting bigger and bigger.

Eventually I realised that this little light was in fact a lot of big lights illuminating a Guest House. I was tired at this point and I did need more fags; also it would be a good idea to find out what the time was. The fact that they sold beer never crossed my mind.

I ordered a drink and looked round for a clock. I couldn't believe it, it was nearly twelve thirty. I panicked, downed my drink and rushed out. Then panicked again as I realised that I hadn't taken much notice of the path from which I had emerged. There were dozens. It took me a while by hit and miss to find the right track.

Eventually I arrived back at camp, and a sergeant got on the walkie-talkie and reported my return to the Major. Unfortunately, he was heading one of the search parties out looking for me. I was told to go and get my head down and I was on report at eight the next morning.

I didn't know it then but our part of the exercise had been cancelled for searches to take place.

On report I explained that I found it almost impossible to find the "end of the track" as instructed, at which the Captain interjected and said that he said "the *bend* of the track". Apparently, half my peers from the tent backed up my version.

Stuart and Wilson had both made statements that they saw me pass them, and even told them what I was singing.

I just got a telling off, but Wilson and Stuart got disciplined for not challenging me while on duty.

It was not long after this incident that I was once again brought before the Major.

He seemed jovial, and in a very upbeat mood, which really surprised me. What he told me was to change my life forever.

"Smith, your application for compassionate discharge has been refused." I was completely shocked, dumbfounded, and very, very angry.

I couldn't believe how heartless and uncaring the Army could be, and it was from that moment on that I decided that I would leave the Army, no matter what.

I have to point out that my application technically was on the right to buy myself out for £200. This option would only be decided on if a good enough reason could be put forward.

The Army's view was that they made it very difficult for any skilled engineer, who had undergone an apprenticeship and rated as 'A' class, to leave the forces, even if their trade, such as mine, were to be made redundant in a short time. If you were rated as 'X' class you had no chance. 'A' class being Electrical or Mechanical, 'X' class being Electronic Engineers.

I mention this fact now as it emphasises what was to happen much later.

Over the next couple of years the MP for Redditch, James Dance, instigated two Ministerial enquiries, the Vicar of Saint Stephens Church wrote numerous letters and my mother and father's Doctor did all he could to help. All to no avail.

I came to the conclusion that one of the barriers against the constant refusals was due to my exemplary record, as barring all my mishaps, on paper I was a model soldier. This I decided had to change.

# Chapter 4
## Winter Warfare

The refusal by the Army to grant me an early release, to buy myself out, hit me hard and left me feeling empty and void of all feelings towards my future in the Army.

I never had much time to dwell on the authorities' decision, as I was soon off again back home as father had taken a turn for the worse.

It wasn't long after that that I was off again on compassionate leave, and this time I had no intention of going back. So by not returning on the due date, I was officially listed as absent without leave (AWOL).

It was only a few days later that a local Policeman came to our house with an arrest warrant, and took me to the local station.

This was the first time that I had ever felt like a celebrity. The reason was that during all that time, which was three days, when I was held at the station, I had a constant stream of constables visiting my cell. Each one turned up with a present of either a hot sandwich, confectionary or the like, and always with a steaming cuppa. I was even woken up during the night, with policemen coming off shift, bearing gifts and wanting a chat.

It had taken a couple of visits before I realised why I was the centre of attention.

Mrs Goodhall's sweet shop was in the street in which I grew up. And also gave lodging to a good many of the towns single policemen.

I was adopted as an unwanted baby, and arguably the first black resident of Redditch, having been born there, which gave me a certain celebrity status.

Over the years and during my boyhood and youth, the ones that married moved into police married quarters, but always kept in touch with Mrs Goodhall. Over those years they had interacted with me, but I hardly knew them.

They knew my history and just wanted a catch up. They also pointed out the errors of my ways and the consequences of going AWOL, and the pressure it would be putting on my parents.

So instead of waiting for a Military escort, which would have been the norm, it was arranged for me to return to Germany under my own recognisance, with the police giving their assurance. I felt that I couldn't let them down, and returned to camp.

I got off relatively lightly with just a week's loss of privileges, or so I thought, but I never realised what the Major also had in store for me.

Before I could plan my next move of disobedience, the Major requested my attendance. He then informed me that I, along with five others, were going to be the unit's six volunteers to go on a winter warfare course to be held in St Andrewsberg. I believe this is where they held the 1938 Winter Olympics.

When I left his office, I told our training officer, Captain Fielding "it's for volunteers so I ain't doing it."

Captain Fielding tried to explain that there would be plenty of men jumping at the chance to learn to ski. Once you get to understand the Army's way of thinking, you get to realise that learning to ski their way is firstly climbing mountains with full kit and ski's. Chair lifts are for sissies. I appreciate that someday it could be an advantage to be able to sleep out in the snow, and survive on a box of hard tack biscuits for a week, but no thanks I'll pass.

So I said, "If you send me, I will make sure that I get kicked off within 48 hours, and that will look bad for the Unit."

He said, "I'm sure you will enjoy it once you get there, but you are definitely going."

I thought perhaps he had eaten too many funny mushrooms by accident.

As a punishment, I along with 5 others were forced into going on the winter warfare course, which was supposed to be for volunteers only. The six of us all put money into a kitty, with the winner being the one who got kicked off first. On the second day I refused to go out on the piste, and was sent to see the Commandant. He explained in no uncertain terms that if he were to send me back, then a letter would be sent to my commanding officer stating that '*this man lacks moral fibre,*' and this would have a detrimental effect on my Army career. I saw this as a plus. I won and Curley asked me how I did it. I said that I told the Commandant to stick the course up his backside.

Curly came back 2 days later, under escort, and was put immediately into the guardhouse. Apparently, he took my wording literally.

It was a matter of days after Curley was released that the Major sent for me again.

I was marched into his office, and instead of being told to "stand at ease" by the Major, he just said, "Smith, your father died last night. Travel documents have been prepared, Dismiss." He never even took a breath.

Although it was news that I had been expecting, it still left me devastated, and my hatred for the Army at that moment knew no bounds. It was then that I realised I couldn't continue in the forces, no matter what the consequences.

I let it be known amongst my friends and comrades that I had no intention of coming back after the funeral. I had no plans as to where to go or what I would do. I knew I could not stay with my mother, even though I wanted to.

She was a child of the Victorian era, and had spent most of her early life in service below stairs. Anyone in a uniform she would kowtow to: postman, gas metre man, so I knew I wouldn't last more than a day at home before she turned me in.

My saviour came from the most unusual source that I could have ever imagined.

I will call him Leslie, and he caused me the biggest trauma in my life that still affects me even now from time to time, but I try not to dwell on it.

As I previously said, there were six of us who had been posted to Osnabruck from the college at Arborfield. Five of us had grown into men together from our early start in junior company. We were like brothers, Baz being a bit of an oddball.

I knew that he stretched the patience of the other four at times, but still we all got on relatively well considering, and I felt as close to him as I did the others. At times I knew that my keeping the peace wasn't always welcome.

Unfortunately, Leslie had failed his trade exams, and was relegated back a division, then passed his tests and was posted out to Germany with us.

From the outset it was obvious that he and Baz never got on, and his intolerance of Baz's stories caused a great deal of bitterness.

Now I must state that I really liked Leslie just as much as I did all our merry little band. He was very popular and had a sharp wit, which we all loved, and he never seemed to have a bad bone in his body. If he had, what he did next would not have been so traumatic to me.

As was our custom we would all go downtown on a Friday night, and hit all the lively bars, including the forbidden red light areas. As there were six of us, it was usual to use two taxies. Leslie had arranged for the both of us to go earlier, and the rest to follow.

What happened next would have done justice to a Hitchcock movie.

We had just got our first beer, and leaning forward in his chair, Leslie said without any tone of malice, "We have always got on, and I don't want to discuss it, especially tonight, but I am going to turn the others against you."

I remember being at first not so much shocked, but more taken aback. Then laughing and waiting for the punch line. It never came. All I remember is him shrugging his shoulders, so I reasoned that what he had said was purely to get a reaction out of me.

I was a bit apprehensive when the others turned up, but everything seemed as normal. Much, much later and after a good many drinks, I brought up in a light manner what Leslie had said.

The minute I repeated our conversation, it was as if a starting gun had gone off.

No words had been said; it was as if they had been waiting for me to mention it, and their physical attack on me was instant. The only thing I remember was their accusation that I was trying to turn them against Leslie.

I was dumbfounded. When I thought about it days later, after we had all but made up, with Leslie being the peace maker, I realised how clever he was, as my future defence of Baz was certainly curtailed. Nothing else made sense.

Anyhow it was Leslie who stepped up to the plate with a suggestion as to where to go AWOL to avoid the Army. So with his promise of help, my future was shaped.

Leslie was going to be on home leave in Bradford a week after my father's funeral, so we arranged to meet up in his home town on a certain date.

Whether he did this out of friendship, or spite, I will never know.

So the die was cast. After the funeral and the granted compassionate leave, I would meet up with Leslie in Bradford.

He had found me lodgings in an ethnic area of Bradford, and to my great surprise, one of his friends had even found me a casual job as a stagehand at the Alhambra theatre. The only down side was that the job wouldn't start until Boxing Day, the start of the pantomime season. The up side was that it was cash in hand.

# Chapter 5
## Alhambra

On that weekend in Bradford with Leslie and his mates, we had a great time and I loved the City and the people I met. I was actually looking forward to going absent.

Leslie however convinced me to go back down to Bordon and at least start the course, as I would only be killing time in Bradford, waiting to start work at the theatre. It made sense, so I said my goodbyes, and told Leslie that I would see him next week when the course started.

It was great meeting up with all my old peers again at Bordon for retraining

It was soon apparent that the majority of the twenty or so of us were very disgruntled, and felt that our apprenticeship had been a waste of time, and we all enjoyed our trade as vehicle electricians. The Army was forcing us to become Airframe and Engines students. To be honest, none of us really knew what the job or opportunity was about, and we were to learn more about it the following Monday, after we had all settled in

Although I empathised with them, it didn't really bother me, as I had set my sights on leaving the Army.

Feelings were running pretty high, and rebellion was in the air.

That weekend we all went out en-masse, and decided to let the Army know just how we felt, and that we wanted more of a choice as to which trade to apply for.

I stayed out of the discussion pretty much, but the consensus was that we were going to 'down tools' so to speak, and refuse to start the course until the powers that be had heard our grievances.

So, on the Monday, with all our hearts and minds made up to rebel, we entered the classroom, and informed the instructor that we wanted a meeting with the training officer to discuss our options. I stayed silent. As I have said, my plans were different to those of my peers.

After a short while Captain Grove entered, and I felt sorry for him as he was one of the few officers that I not only liked but highly respected.

He gave our proposals a fair hearing, and laid the down consequences. Acting against Queen's Regulations would be considered mutinous and punishment would be harsh and severe.

His honest and direct speech, given in absolute silence, was delivered, and if he had then given the class some time to dwell on his words and sum up the implications of our actions, then my future may have taken a different course

He then asked us individually what we wanted to do, either stay on the course or opt out.

Once again I was in the wrong place at the wrong time. Being basically a shy person I always tried to sit at the back of classes. On this occasion my seat was at the back in the corner on the left.

He started with me, and out of loyalty to my mates plus the fact that I was seated next to one of the ringleaders of the mutiny I said, "No, I want off."

Nick Besant shook me when he elected to stay.

From then on it was just like a pack of cards tumbling, everyone followed his lead.

I have never felt more let down before or since in my life.

The very next day, I was on orders to see our Company Commander, Major Hurst, who was seconded from the Canadian Army. He shocked me when he said that arrangements had been made to transfer me back to 12 Infantry workshops, where the Mad Major was in charge. My flight was the forthcoming Friday.

I had never been so depressed, and pleaded with him to send me anywhere but back to Osnabruck.

He listened to my pleas with a genuine look of sympathy. Turning to the Sergeant who was standing behind him he said "This lad's been through hell. It's about time that he had a break. Cancel Friday's flight. We will try and get him a different posting."

I was so pleased I could have kissed him.

That night the Major's Sergeant, along with the same Staff Sergeant from the clerk's office, who had shook my hand and welcomed me to Bordon on the day I had arrived, paid me a visit.

They sat on my bed and the Staff Sergeant gave me an envelope with my posting orders.

I was to catch the next available flight back to Osnabruck, which was noon the next day. I protested and said to the Sergeant, "You were there, he promised to find me a different posting."

I could feel tears welling up in my eyes. He shook me with his next statement. "As soon as you left the Major's office, he instructed me to get you on the next available flight back to Osnabruck."

Before I could vent my anger the Staff Sergeant said, "That's why I am here, not just to give you your travelling papers, but I am disgusted at how you have been treated. I am here to let you know your rights under Queen's Regulations. It's simple. You have already been posted out of Osnabruck and posted here. It's every soldier's right to be granted a minimum of one week's leave before any posting, but you need to know what Queen's Reg's you need to quote. Major Hurst will have to explain to his seniors why one flight has been cancelled, another one booked and then cancelled again in 48 hours."

So the three of us sat there and drafted my request under the regulations. Then he took possession of the letter to get it authorised first thing the following morning.

My faith in human nature was restored.

The next day Major Hurst sent for me, and said with a tearful look in his eye, "I have checked the Queen's Regulations, and it seems you are right. You are entitled to a week's leave. It will start tomorrow morning, but you won't be coming back here. Your flight to Osnabruck is booked for the day that your leave ends."

Before I could say a word, his face suddenly lit up, and he added, "There is one proviso though. I need you to read this declaration and if you understand it, sign it and go."

I can't remember the exact wording, but in essence it said that if I were to miss my flight to Osnabruck then I could or would be charged with desertion. I signed the paper knowing that I had no intention of catching the intended flight. He knew that as well.

My friendly Staff Sergeant from the clerk's office said it was a shame that I had signed, and then explained that the charge of desertion only applies to soldiers on active service who try to avoid a conflict. In fact, if a soldier went AWOL for a long time, such as 20 years or more, then the chances are he wouldn't be charged for desertion, only AWOL.

So I went home, told mother not to worry and that I would be in touch as soon as I found some digs and a job. Off to Bradford I went. It was mid-December and freezing.

So it came to pass that I was to endure the worst Christmas of my life, but I also entered a magical time, a period that I will never forget.

The downside was that I rented a room in Lastridge Lane, Bradford, arranged by Leslie, as was the part time job at the Alhambra Theatre, where I was to be paid 10 shillings a show as a stage hand during the Pantomime season.

Unfortunately, the panto season started on Boxing Day, which meant that I needed to survive a full week on the couple of pounds I had left. By the time Christmas Day had arrived, I was down to my last half a crown, or if you prefer, two and six in old money. In today's currency it would be about twelve pence.

As if that wasn't bad enough I was suffering from a bad bout of flu, and I truly believed that I would never make it through to Boxing Day.

That Christmas Day I stayed in bed, and put my last shilling in the gas metre.

The only means of heat was a small gas fire. I had already invested in a pack of Spangles (similar to Tunes) to ease my red, raw, sore throat, and that left enough for a packet of crisps for sustenance. This was to be my Christmas.

Boxing Day couldn't come soon enough. I don't remember getting through my illness as I threw myself into the interesting world of the theatre, and meeting the great array of people involved in the making of a show.

I made a lot of friends, not only with the stage staff but some of the players and actors.

One person in particular was a lad of my age, Gary West. His father was a member of the popular Black and White Minstrel show. Not the TV group, but the ones which toured stages around Europe. I left my digs and we rented a flat together which was closer to the Theatre.

The money we earned in a week was never going to be sufficient enough to live on, so we used our wits and charm to get by.

Gary was a great hit with women. The older ones wanted to mother him, and regularly brought him pies and the like, and the younger ones wouldn't see him go without money or a night out, and I was always included.

For my part, I found myself warding off the attentions of two of the cast of Robin Hood's merry men, who were a part of the *Babes in the Wood* pantomime.

Although I had made it very clear that I wasn't gay in any shape or form, they both seemed to compete for my attention. One regularly made a stew for me and Gary, whilst the other supplied fabulous curries. Our staple diet was usually omelettes, which I provided through my job in the prop room.

Anyone who has watched a pantomime with an ugly Dame in the cast, such as Widow Twankey, will probably remember the scenes where she hides eggs inside her bra, and inevitably some actor manages to accidentally fall against her, breaking them in the process. Well, it was a part of my job to ensure the eggs were empty, so I spent a little amount of time blowing the innards into a bowl, which I took back to our digs each night. This provided our breakfast each morning.

During this time in Bradford I met one of the most influential people I have ever met. His name was Bob Carlisle, the biggest extrovert one could imagine.

Being quite shy and introverted most of my life, becoming friends with him had to affect me and my outlook changed completely.

It would be simpler to retell the story than to try and explain what he was all about. Most of the time we would meet in the Student's Union bar of the college. He may have been the Chairman of the Student's Union, or on the committee; anyhow, everybody knew him.

One night he suggested we go out and paint the town red as he wanted to celebrate his exam results. We all pleaded poverty, but he said, "No matter," so off we went, thinking that he had come into money. This was far from the truth.

I should point out that this was a time of major crisis between India and Pakistan over Kashmir.

The four of us followed him into a pub frequented by Sikhs. We walked up to the bar where a group of turban wearing men were stood having a drink. Before the barmaid came to serve us, Bob turned to the Sikhs and asked them if they were Pakistanis, to which they replied "No!"

Quick as a flash he said, "Good, we are all on your side in this conflict," and followed it up with a few disparaging words against the Pakistani government, and asked if we could buy them a drink. They insisted on buying *us* a drink. After quite a few free beers, he made an excuse for us to leave as we needed to be somewhere urgently.

He had certainly done his homework, because in a matter of minutes we were in a predominately Pakistani pub where he went through the same routine, but in reverse.

I lost count how many pubs he executed this con in, but oh what a night!

I imagine everyone has at least one moment in life that they can look back on and feel immensely proud. Mine came whilst working in the Alhambra theatre.

The stars of the show, *Babes in the Wood*, were Mike and Bernie Winters. A scandal hit the theatre when it was realised that a member of the cast, or one of the backstage staff, was a thief. Valuables, but mainly money, was being stolen from the dressing rooms. The police were brought in and interviewed everyone, except for me. It was common knowledge that I was AWOL from the Army. When I say common knowledge, I don't include Mike and Bernie in that, but their road manager, Mike, certainly knew, as did the management of the theatre. In fact, the police did spot checks, which were very regular (rumour was, they were looking for me). The actors including the Corp De Ballet used to hide me on stage in one of the props whenever they could.

Apparently, the cash amounts being stolen were relatively small and were still being executed after the police interviews. Then it happened the wages of the two stars were taken; we found out later that their money was used as bait, and was tainted with a special dye. Again, I was kept under wraps when the police used their infra-red detector on everyone. The culprit was caught, and turned out to be the doorman who had worked there for nearly twenty years.

Can you imagine how I felt during all this. Instead of being the main suspect, everyone had that much faith in me.

Talking about faith, and being quite a religious person, I went to see the Bishop of Bradford, the Right Reverend Parker, at his home. I explained my plight to him in the hope that he might be able to help, but he seemed more concerned about how I found his residence. After a very short meeting he said, "I can't help you as I don't know you."

I remember getting up and going to the door, turning and saying, "It's a good job Jesus didn't have the same point of view as you." I realised later how unfair the remark was. Maybe I let something slip concerning my wherabouts, which is why the police were so persistent on calling into the theatre at all hours.

There was one other person backstage that I often think about. For the purpose of this story we will call him Bill.

Bill was only 17, and worked part time as a bouncer at different establishments because he lied about his age. He lived for fighting, wasn't interested in girls or beer one little bit, so it was strange that he hung out with us.

I remember one day we were having something to eat in one of our local cafes when in came two men who looked Asian. Bill looked excited and said, "Hey, lets go and do 'em over."

I asked, "Why?"

He said, "Because they're black."

I couldn't believe it as I had never taken him to be a racist. I then said, "Hang on, I'm black, if not blacker than either of them."

He wouldn't have it, but I could never get him to accept that I was black. I distanced myself from him when I heard that he and another friend of his went to an evening pantomime show carrying light bulbs. For a laugh they were throwing them on stage from high up in the circle, and one of the bulbs caused damage to Mike Winters.

The authorities eventually found out not only where I was working but where I lived. This came about because of a friend who I had met earlier in my Army career. He decided that he would join me in Bradford. His name was Keith, and he had promised me that he wouldn't let his family know where we were. However, he did tell his brother and the rest is history.

We were held in the Bradford cells awaiting an Army escort, which was to arrive the following day. Next morning, all the new prisoners were taken out of the cells, so that the shift of the day could get a good look at everyone and take note of what we were wearing. I told Keith to be prepared to "do a runner," if and when I thought the time was right.

I told him to listen out for me saying, "Bob Carlisle. If I say Bob, then be prepared, and when I say Carlisle, then run."

What happened next would have been worthy of a spot on *You've Been Framed!*

We couldn't do much with both the police and the three Army escorts taking us to the station, nor could we attempt an escape from the train, but as we came into Waterloo station it just felt right. I only hoped Keith had remembered the code.

The five of us disembarked from the train and stood there waiting for a while.

Then the NCO in charge of the escort said, "Watch them, I'm going to get the tickets."

I realised this was our best chance, so I said to Keith, "I wonder what Bob's doing now." I was sure his ears pricked up, so I went on, "You know, Bob Carlisle." At this point Keith and I were facing each other, about five feet apart

We both slung our kitbags at the soldiers closest to us and darted.

In a split second the kitbags landed on the ground, I managed to jump over mine and made a dash to the stairs leading down to the road. Keith wasn't so lucky. He jumped over his bag, realised that I had passed him, turned and fell over my bag, bringing down the two escorts. When I glanced back, I was nearly doubled up with laughter until I saw a couple of PCs heading my way, and the NCO had joined the chase.

What happened next really went in my favour. As I was bounding down the steps and turning a corner to tackle the next flight, I noticed a little girl of about 3 or 4 trip and tumble. Without thinking I stopped to pick her up and console her, as she was hysterical. By the time my pursuers had advanced on me, it must have looked as though I had knocked her over. The Constables and the NCO then took statements from onlookers and the mother, who all praised me for my actions.

It wasn't until my Courts Martial that I was made aware of the glowing reports made by the witness statements.

# Chapter 6
## Psychiatrist and Courts Martial

The Army escort finally delivered us to the camp at Bordon in Hampshire.

To be honest, I felt relieved that it was all over, and that I could be punished and gladly accept my dismissal from the Army.

Fate played a nasty trick on me, as when the escort was signing me over to the duty Guard House Regimental Police, the Corporal of the guard said in a sneering way, "Seems like you're quite a celebrity. I believe Colonel Lawless is looking forward to renewing his acquaintance with you."

It felt that my spine had turned to ice, my legs went wobbly, and I could hardly ask the question, "You don't mean Major Lawless from Osnabruck?" They answered in the affirmative, and added that he had been promoted to Lieutenant Colonel.

They showed me to my cell, fetched me some food from the cookhouse, and said as a passing shot, "We will bring your uniform in the morning as you are up in front of the Colonel tomorrow afternoon."

This filled me with dread and consternation, and that night I couldn't sleep worrying as to what was going to happen.

I came up with the most stupid idea that I ever had. It was on par with General Custer's decision to take the 7th cavalry to the "*Little Big Horn,* to teach Sitting Bull a lesson."

I decided not to play the Army game anymore and that when they brought my uniform, I would refuse to accept it. This I did the next morning.

What happened next really surprised me. The Army's reaction to my stand was complete indifference. This lasted for over 90 days.

They brought my food, exercised me, and were polite, but nobody tried to persuade me or order me to do anything.

I was later told that 94 days was a record for someone to be under close arrest without being charged.

Two months in and I admit that I did breakdown in my cell. I could see out of the bars of the cell all the inhabitants of the camp leaving to go on their two week Easter break. It wasn't just that which filled me with sadness, it was the fact that it was my birthday.

After another month went by, my mind and reasoning was changed by a duty sergeant. I asked him how long he thought my present position would last, why no officer had shown their face, or why no one had tried to order me about.

His reply was that nothing would happen whilst I was refusing to soldier.

It took me less than a week to put on my uniform and give in to what the future held for me.

The Regimental Police in the Guard House, who had waited on me and served my every need with courtesy and politeness, showed their true colours. The next weeks were hell, and every conceivable dirty task imaginable was heaped on me from dusk to dawn, but they never broke my spirit.

I had one welcoming face which I never expected. It was the Sergeant from Major Hurst's office.

He had come to tell me that he would be more than willing to give evidence at my Courts Martial as to the way I was treated and lied to. He was referring to my acceptance of being subjected to a Courts Martial should I fail to return for my flight.

He explained he would have served his 22 year service in a matter of weeks, and he at least wouldn't have me on his conscience when he was in Civvie Street. He also reiterated what many a person had said to me, that people in very high office were watching the outcome of my career.

This filled me with hope, but that hope was shattered a few weeks later.

Colonel Lawless showed his hatred towards me by not setting a courts martial date until I underwent a series of tests and examinations. One of these examinations was a series of tests to see if I was mentally sound.

He was worried that I would use the defence of 'not being of sound mind' at my trial.

He was determined to throw the book at me!

One of the last psychiatric examinations was by a Colonol psychiatrist, and I thought this is my chance of turning the tables back on the CO.

I had always had the idea of entering the acting fraternity, and here was my chance. If I could pull this off, then I would certainly consider trying to get into RADA.

Who wouldn't want to be a film star?

I did a lot of practising in my cell preparing for my performance, such as remembering to stammer continuously, whilst not only blinking and shifting my eyes from object to object, but also getting into the habit of not finishing sentences, and going off at a tangent into nonsensical stories. I found wringing my hands as I spoke added that little bit of spice to the proceedings.

Of course, having an imaginary friend come into the conversation from time to time was a part of my act when I was at a loss for words, but not over doing it was key. I realised that I had to leave the odd gaps of sanity in the conversation to play on his sympathy, and make it more realistic.

I was booked in for a one hour session, but the first session went on for over two hours, and the second appointment took most of a morning with occasional breaks.

I felt that we had actually become very good friends. I also felt that I had passed my audition with flying colours. RADA, here I come!

There were no more sessions booked, and I was left wondering what was going to happen next.

Of course, back at the guardhouse I had to keep up the act as I realised that the Regimental Police would have to put in their reports. I was only glad that I had practised for weeks before, and using different techniques only helped my cause as it would seem that I had deteriorated over a period of time.

After a few days, I was summoned back. Off I went back under escort, and was shown into the now familiar office. The escorts had left, and I stood there for a while, realising that I may still be under surveillance. I continued with my fruitcake act.

Eventually the Doctor entered the room, asked me to sit down and what happened next I would regret for the rest of my life.

He just sat there at his desk, occasionally looking up, sometimes with the odd friendly smile. Not a word was said.

Without warning he suddenly stood up, outstretched his hand. For a high ranking officer to do this completely threw me off balance

Without thinking, I stood and shook his hand, and he said with a smile, "Congratulations, you nearly had me."

Now this is what I regret. I should have carried on the act, but instead I just smiled.

He called the escorts back in, and I was whisked away, knowing that the date for the courts martial would soon be set. I did like him though.

In fact, up until that point he was only the second officer in the Army that I had ever liked or respected. The other officer I was about to be reunited with under the worst of circumstances.

The date for the trial was set, and I wondered if an officer would automatically be appointed, or if I would have to defend myself. As the appointed date grew closer I worried that no defence officer had approached me.

With three days to go, a very young officer about my age, early twenties, arrived at the Guard Room. He was straight out of Sandhurst, and his child like mentality really worried me. I would like to be kind and say "Nice but dim", but no. Just dim!

I think he said he had volunteered for the job as my defence lawyer. To him it was just a game.

He never took any notes, which concerned me greatly. When I pointed it out, he was flippant, and said he had all the facts of my case files, but wouldn't divulge what was in them.

I thought I would pass on the information about Major Hurst's sergeant volunteering to give evidence at my trial. He looked shocked, and this was the only time that he took out a little notebook and jotted any information down.

He left quickly, and I was surprised when he returned a couple of hours later.

I don't know who he went to see, but he was agitated and told me that he had been advised to tell me that if I brought an officer's name into disrepute, then the courts would come down on me like a ton of bricks, and my sentence would be severe.

I began feeling sorry for him. When he started begging and pleading with me to withdraw my defence, I reluctantly agreed. That was the last I saw of him until judgement day.

The Courts Martial for desertion was a joke, and I barely remember much about it; it would have done an episode of Monty Python proud.

I was shocked to find that the appointed prosecution officer was the first officer that I had ever come to like and respect. It was Captain Grove and he was Major Hurst's second in command. He looked very uneasy stating the Army's case against me; it was obvious he didn't want to be there, and looked strained trying to blacken my name. He hardly looked at me, but just stood there addressing the three high ranking Staff Officers. He finished presenting the case, and only then as he was sitting down did he look at me, with a look that said, "Sorry."

The reason I remember very little was because the Second Lieutenant, who was my defence, was told to submit my case.

There he was, slouched back on his chair, not exactly legs crossed, but laid so far back, with his right foot resting on his left knee. He started addressing the three Judges. One of the judges went berserk at the contempt he was showing the court, then another judge joined in. The dressing down he got was out of this world.

Everyone in court was shook at the ferocity of the judges, except of course for my defence. He seemed impervious to any criticism and seemed to be enjoying his moment in the spotlight.

I, at this point, realised that all was lost and it made me lose all interest in the proceedings. Most of the trial ended up with the three judges nit picking on everything the Lieutenant said or did.

All I remember was the sentence given of 84 days confinement at the correction centre situated in Colchester, the Army's Alcatraz.

I was marched out and taken the five minute drive back to the guard room. It was at this point that I now believed that powerful higher ups were indeed following my career. On arriving back we were informed that the Commanding Officer of the Southern region had reduced my internment to 70 days.

This decision was made and executed all in 5 minutes.

# Chapter 7
## Military Corrective Training Establishment

The MCTE at Colchester was a real eye opener. I thought the glass house was bad, but looking back it was a holiday camp compared to the regime I now found myself in.

Colchester houses inmates from every Regiment in the British Army. Most who pass through there are dishonourably discharged after finishing their sentence. I wasn't so lucky.

There was another unfortunate inmate that I had heard about the first week I was there; he was also not given a dishonourable discharge from the Army. He achieved the almost impossible, and somehow escaped from the camp. His intention wasn't to get away, rather to be recaptured quickly, but that never happened. He hadn't thought it through properly, so he improvised.

He stole a car and drove around the town most of the day in the hope of being caught, but to no avail. Then his luck changed as it was getting dark.

He saw a police panda car, and no matter how many times he overtook it on the road, he still wasn't being pulled over. In desperation he decided to fake an accident, and rammed the police car.

When they brought him back, he was sent to the dreaded 'C' wing, where rumour had it, the only clothing issued was a canvas boiler suit.

I never did get to meet him, as he was still in 'C' wing when I left. I always wondered if he achieved his aim of being dismissed.

There were only two other soldiers from my corps, the REME, doing time, and one of them was well acquainted with some of the antics which had blighted my career.

To be fair, I had also heard of the misdemeanour which had brought him here. That too had circulated far and wide.

He was initially a good, text book soldier, stationed in the Middle East at Aden.

One day he had gone down to the local town in a Land Rover as a part of his duties. He and the person he was with decided to pop into a bar used by squaddies off duty for a quick drink before making their way back to camp.

Unfortunately, when they came out, the Land Rover had been stolen. Knowing the mindset of the Arabs, it was a hard and fast rule that one person should always stay with a vehicle when out of camp. Their punishment was quite lenient considering.

He was much more careful on future trips for weeks to come.

A couple of months later, he was approached by an Arab, who apologised for getting him into trouble by stealing his vehicle, and suggested that they could put matters right. He gave him a wad of money, but offered him twice as much if he could accidentally leave the keys in the ignition of the jeep.

He jumped at the chance, waved the Arab off and went in search of his comrade under some pretext, with the intention of looking surprised at the missing jeep.

Unfortunately, when they got back to camp, as well as filling in his report they asked him for the vehicle keys, as they did the first time it had happened. Not having them, but instead having such a large stash of money was his downfall. Plus, the rumours circulating amongst the Arab community didn't help.

The day came soon enough for my release, and although I was ecstatic about being free, I stood there on the platform at Colchester station with my newly issued travel documents, which would whisk me back to the camp at Bordon. The immediate problem in my mind was whether I should go, or take another unauthorised holiday. The recent experiences of the MCTE fresh in my mind helped me make my decision, so I was soon on my way back.

My big disappointment on returning to camp was the fact that after my four months AWOL, my prolonged spell in the Guard Room, and my recent internment meant that all my old compadres had finished their upgrade and were posted on to various units around the globe. It took me a few days to recover from my despondency.

My biggest surprise of all was the change in the way the Army treated me. It was almost surreal, and it seemed that everyone was under orders to not upset me, and I do mean everyone, NCOs and officers alike.

I never had a role to play, as it was a training camp, and I soon realised that because the Army had changed its mind in making electricians redundant and was about to start a retraining programme for them, I was to bide my time and wait for a new posting. I became a gofer, handyman, or just a spare part in the great scheme of things. They even issued me with a bicycle to get around on.

I was pretty much left to my own devices, just a few odd jobs, but my main duty was delivering mail to the four separate company offices, and also listing HQ's orders and information on company notice boards.

Colonel Lawless, Major Hurst, the Staff Sergeant from the Clerk's Office, and the Sergeant from Major Hurst's office, who wanted to give evidence on my behalf, had all vanished, and I never saw any of them again.

It's hard to visualise how I was treated during this time, but there was a situation which aptly shows how things were.

As any soldier would tell you, there are morning inspections in all barrack rooms for cleanliness and neatness, especially in training establishments. One morning I overslept, but I was awakened by the sound of voices and footsteps down the corridor. In a flash, panic set in as I recognised the voices of the Company Sergeant Major and my CO. I shot out of bed and realised I hadn't time to make my bed up in the regulated way, so I hastily threw it together. It was a mess, but I had a choice to either leave it or get caught in the barrack room, which would make a bad situation worse. I gathered my boots and beret and carried on dressing as I left the room via the Fire Exit.

Outside I looked at my watch and realised that I had missed morning parade by at least an hour. *Here we go again* I thought, and waited to be called to book during the rest of the day. It never happened, but what happened the next day surprised me even more.

I was determined not to miss the next day's parade, but at the end of it, when the parade was dismissed for the soldiers to attend their classes, the duty Sergeant called me back, told me to collect all my kit and belongings and meet him outside the barrack block in an hour. The feeling of trepidation swept over me as I realised that I was about to remake my acquaintance with the guard room.

I was surprised that although I was loaded down with bed clothes, Army kit and two suit cases, he helped me by carrying the suit cases, and he took me to another block and showed me into a single room, reserved normally for NCOs.

This is where I stayed for the rest of my duration. I missed many morning Parades over the next few weeks, without any comeback. Eventually, I gave up attending altogether.

I felt that I was becoming a Sgt Bilko type figure, a mister fix-it. No wonder they moved me away from the raw recruits; it couldn't have done much for their morale.

During one of my daily postings of events and information on the company's notice boards, there was one official listing concerning the forthcoming annual Queen's Birthday Parade.

The notice was to inform all ranks that there would be no leave allowed on the weekend of the Parade, unless there were exceptional circumstances. Anyone who felt that they had a good reason to be excused from the forthcoming parade should apply to their company Commanding Officer before a certain date.

I was never a fan of the bullshit side of Army life, especially parades.

I immediately devised a plan of action. They wouldn't allow too many absentees at one time, so I didn't post the missive until I had my application approved.

The guards on the camp gates were used to my frequent comings and goings in and out of the camp on my trusty bike. Up to the local village shop I sped, and bought a pack of wedding invitations.

I carefully filled it out for the weekend of the parade, but I needed that extra step to give it more credence. I asked the

Company Sergeant Major for an audience with the CO, which was granted. I explained that although I'd had the invitation for some time, there had now been a change. The best man could no longer make it, and I was asked to step in, to which I had accepted.

One problem, I told him, was that I would also be needed a couple of days before, to fulfil my duties properly, such as church rehearsals, organising stag night etc. This he accepted and gave me approval then and there. I soon put up the company notices to give others a chance for the weekend off. I managed to sell all the left over wedding invitation cards within a few days and made a handsome profit. Result!

# Chapter 8
## Iserlohn

It wasn't long after this that I was informed that a posting had been found for me.

Although I hadn't stopped trying to obtain my Army release on compassionate grounds, I realised that maybe a different perspective might become apparent if I was located in a different surrounding. I looked forward to a change of scenery.

My posting was to 50 Missile Regiment in a small town in Germany called Minden, near the town of Iserlohn.

It was more of a support unit, unlike the major workshops, with all the bull and regimentation associated with them. This place had a good feel about it, but that feeling was soon to be squashed.

My first port of call, as any soldier would do, was a visit to the clerk's office to pick up my booking in form. With this form one was to go to the Quarter Masters store for bedding, the armoury to be issued with a rifle and etc.

Everyone in the clerk's office seemed friendly enough, and I chatted to the four men and they made me feel welcome.

Then all hell broke loose. At one end of the clerk's office there was a doorway and the door was slightly ajar, and just as the chief clerk handed me my form that he had just signed, there was a sharp cry of "No, No", and the door was jerked open wide. Standing there in the doorframe looking like he had just been shot was my new CO Captain Fielding, Major Lawless's second in command at Osnabruck.

He stood there ranting at me, saying, "Whatever you do, do not book in." In fact, he snatched the form out of my hand. "I'm not having you here," he screamed.

I learnt days later that no one had ever seen him in that sort of state before; he normally was very placid.

I just stood there, more embarrassed than angry, and my immediate thought was how unlucky I had been. What, with of all the hundreds of postings worldwide, would be the chance of this happening. Maybe someone high up in the Army had a really sick sense of humour.

Anyway, I couldn't see him when he went back into his office, but he screamed out to the Sergeant in charge of the clerk's office, "Get him issued with some emergency bedding and that's all. Smith, don't you dare unpack, you will be out of here within days."

The Sergeant gently put his hand on my shoulder, and said, "Come on lad, we'll get you sorted."

What I remember most about the encounter was, as we were leaving the office, the Captain screaming down the phone, "I've been lumbered, no I'm not having it, I've been lumbered." I don't know who he was talking to.

They showed me to a two man room, and this I shared with a soldier called 'Shorty'. He wasn't particularly short in stature, it was because his surname was Short. By the time that I had left this camp, we had become very good friends.

For a couple of days I hung around doing nothing. The old adage is that the Devil finds work for idle hands.

As I have said I was still trying to blacken my name, to give the Army a good enough reason to get rid of me. It didn't take me long to come up with a plan, and I was in the perfect place to put it into operation. In reality, it was because I was now attached to a Missile Regiment that gave me the idea.

I joined the CND (Campaign for Nuclear Disarmament), and asked them to send me not only information, but posters for me to put up locally.

After a few days the Captain sent for me and informed me that he was stuck with me for the near future. He read me the riot act, but said he would give me a fair chance. He said he didn't have much option, as electricians were few and far between. I was so relieved and pleased.

I felt at home here. It was a tightly knit body of men: one officer, an ASM, three or four sergeants and about thirty NCOs and other ranks. We were like one big happy family, and I could have quite happily stayed there for ever had I not had my mother's welfare always at the back of my mind.

This must have been the most laid back posting in the whole of the British Army. I fitted in straight away. Everyone, from the CO down through the ranks seemed to have the same mentality, to do your job to the best of your ability, and not to worry about the bullshit normally associated with being a soldier.

The workshop was a relatively small rectangular building about 75 metres by 30. On the second floor were the offices and our own fairly large Social Club, which was used by almost everyone on a daily basis.

I remember an instance when the Captain took an early morning stroll around the workshop. This wasn't abnormal in itself, but what was unusual was the fact that he made sure that he spoke to everyone, even if only for a brief moment, then disappeared upstairs to his office.

After a short time he came back down from his office and stood on the bottom steps, blew a whistle, held up a piece of paper, then when he was sure he had everyman's attention, he loudly announced, "All ranks must read this Order that he would put on the notice board, before they stopped work for dinner."

The notice announced that the ASM felt that there was a feeling of low morale amongst the troops when he walked through the workshop that morning.

The Captain went on to say that he agreed with him after conducting his own brief survey.

There certainly wasn't a low morale amongst us. It was true that none of us were at our perkiest that morning, as we all had a late and heavy night downtown the previous evening and were suffering hangovers.

The notice went on, that work would stop an hour earlier than usual, at 4 pm, and our club would be open to accommodate all those who wished to have a social drink. Those that didn't want to partake would be required to carry on working.

It went on that this would be the norm everyday until further notice, until morale had been restored.

Most soldiers have to do a yearly classification on armaments, but in REME being a good engineer is paramount. We weren't issued with arms, but still had to go to the range for classification on rifles.

It was so embarrassing when only a handful passed the tests. The ASM argued the point with the Captain that it was a particularly windy and blustery day. Reluctantly our CO agreed and so the scores were doubled. This still meant that over 50% of us had failed, but we never had to redo the test.

God, did I love this place!

On the personal front, I have never had so many close friends in my life as I did there, with three men in particular. Apart from Shorty from Leicester, there was Spike from Manchester and Cliff from Ledbury. We were inseparable.

One night we were downtown drinking in our favourite bars, which happened to be the 'Off Limits' establishments, when we got into an altercation with a large group of locals, and although we were heavily outnumbered at the beginning, a group of gunners from the artillery unit we were stationed at joined in to even up the numbers.

It's hard to explain, but it may have been due to the amount of drink we had consumed and our adversaries being in the same state that the fight was really enjoyable.

Then something very unusual happened. In the middle of the affray I glimpsed a knife in someone's hand, and so did one of the Germans. He and I both started shouting above the noise of the brawl, "There's a knife, someone's got a knife!"

The fighting stopped in a matter of seconds, and both we and the Germans wanted to know who had introduced a knife. We never did find out, and we all shook hands and bid our farewells.

It was all very surreal.

The next weekend we heard that the same group of Germans were looking for us, so we were on our guard everywhere we went.

It wasn't until after midnight that they came into the Guest House, where we nearly always finished the night with a meal. There were only three of them, but we reckoned the rest were not far away, probably outside waiting.

They were smiling and pro-offered their hands, like all Germans do, pulled up some chairs, and bought a round of drinks for the four of us. They then began telling us how much they had enjoyed the fight the other night and how they respected us, especially concerning the knife incident.

The reason they had been looking for us for the past couple of weeks was that they were hoping that we would join them in a prearranged fight that they had set up against a group from a neighbouring town. Of course we declined the offer.

I personally had a big scare whilst at 50 Missile workshop. I felt I had really settled in, but as I said before, although I was enjoying my life and still was keeping my hopes alive of being compassionately discharged, I had toned down my pro-activities of disobedience.

My scare came when I realised that I still had a mountain of CND literature hidden in my locker, so I decided to dump them.

My one concern was that I never wanted them found on the campus, so my plan was to take them in my Herbie type Volkswagen (well it was jointly owned by Shorty) and dump them downtown in a skip. The artillery guardsmen on the gate never gave those of us in REME any grief and always waved us through.

The plan was to carry them in a large plastic shopping bag to my car, which was parked on the main car park shared by all. Inside the bag the leaflets were bundled up with elastic bands.

I had waited for the next Sunday morning when it would be quiet, and slipped out of our barrack block and took a short walk to the car park. I made a mistake by taking a short cut through the bushes which formed a border.

Unfortunately, the bag snagged on the branches, ripping it apart. It wouldn't have been so bad except that one of the elastic bands had snapped, and before I realised what was happening, about a dozen posters were caught by the blustery wind, circulated in the air and were blown every which way. I chased after them, but more escaped from the torn bag.

Panic set in when I heard the roar of the engines of a couple heavy transporters turning into the main avenue at the far end of the car park. These large American articulated transporters, commonly known as 'MAC's' were each carrying an 'Honest John Missile' on their trailers. I had no time to retrieve the posters blowing about in the wind. The situation turned grim, as when the Mac's got close to the leaflets their powerful fans behind the radiators pulled the papers towards them. One CND leaflet bearing the symbol was sucked onto the grill, as if strategically placed there by a large but delicate hand. It was not surprising how quickly soldiers had managed to find camera's to capture this unusual, but funny moment.

I jumped into my car and prayed that I had not been seen, more so that no one knew that I had a cache of CND literature and posters.

The unfortunate incident was thoroughly investigated, but mainly concentrated on the artillery quarters at the camp. I lived in limbo for weeks wondering if I would be found to be connected in some way.

Shorty and I had bought our second-hand Beetle Volkswagen with the intention of applying to enter an open rally, run by one of the national newspapers. This rally was to start in England and finish in Mexico to coincide with the start of the football World Cup.

Our CO had given us permission, providing we funded the cost ourselves. We really felt that we were in with a chance, and we had nearly a year to save and prepare ourselves.

Shorty came up with the idea that we should at least put our 'Herbie' car through its paces, by going on a long trip to see if any faults materialised and give us an idea on petrol consumption.

We decided on driving down to Llorett in the Costa Brava, Spain for our summer holidays. We had a fantastic holiday and made numerous friends who I kept in touch with for many years, except for two unusual drifters that we had befriended in the Western Saloon.

One was a clean cut kid, who could have fitted in anywhere, and his travelling companion, a tall lean American hippy, who insisted on calling me Floyd. This name stuck with me for years. He was brash, very outspoken, but before he opened his mouth, one's judgement of him was instantly made because of the very large swastika medallion hung around his neck that dangled like a medal on the outside of his power flower vest.

What was hard to believe was how two complete opposites came to be travelling companions. They explained to us that both their fathers were high ranking officers in the occupational forces stationed in Cologne, which was the American sector of divided Germany. They had hitch hiked down to Llorett for their holidays. The American told us many strange stories about his exploits that took place during his rides with his Hells Angel's Chapter back home.

If he was to be believed, he was there when my hero Bob Dylan nearly lost his life in a motorcycle crash, which nearly ended his career.

I was disappointed when they informed us one night that they were leaving the next morning to hitch back to Germany. They had given themselves two days to make the journey. I tried to talk them into waiting a full three days, which was when me and Shorty were planning on going back, and we could give them a lift all the way to Cologne, as it was on route to Iserlohn.

They couldn't wait as they had promised their respective families that they would return on or by a certain day. We said our farewells with a heavy heart.

We carried on our holiday with the rest of the friends we had met. We both had an obsession with taking a certain memento back with us: a very large billboard advertising a flamenco show. There were two main obstacles in obtaining this billboard. The first was its size; it stood at five feet high and about three feet wide and was made of wood. The second problem was that it was located outside the Town Hall, which also housed the main offices of the Municipal police. Being caught by the police didn't bother us as much as being caught by the machine gun toting Militia.

That really scared us. We knew we needed to be drunk, as it would be put down to high jinx if we were caught, but not too drunk to not be able to carry out our plan.

Around and opposite the Town Hall were several restaurants all with outside diners, but around midnight the waiting staff were more concerned with packing up tables and chairs.

The last night of the holiday came and we were prepared. Our plan seemed so simple.

That last night we had loaded up the car with our suitcases, and most importantly were wearing our clothes for the night out, the same clothes that we would be travelling back to camp in.

Our plan was to park the car on the beachside of the Esplanade, about 50 metres away from the Town Hall, and close to the access leading to the beach.

On the beach were numerous tarpaulin sheets covering up deckchairs and the like. Timing was all important. We waited until midnight knowing that the militia would concentrate their attentions on the drunks, and hang around the liveliest bars and clubs until the early morning.

We would snatch the billboard, take it across the main road, which was the esplanade, and down onto the beach. Then cover it with a tarpaulin sheet, and get up very early next morning, put the prize on the roof rack protected by some cardboard. Then we would get the suitcases out of the car and put them on the back of the sign so as to preserve the picture of the dancers.

The plan went like a dream, and we were on our way out of Llorett by five o'clock.

All we had to do now was worry about the Spanish customs, which were always manned by the dreaded Militia. If caught we had rehearsed our story, that we were drunk one night, and someone had sold it to us.

When we arrived at the customs, I thought my heart was about to burst. We had planned and executed the task while under the influence, but being sober was a different matter. I visualised the next few years of my life being locked up in a Spanish jail. As it happened, we were waved through. I have never felt so relieved, and put my foot down to get as far away from the frontier as possible.

This was a mistake, and nearly brought our escapade to a disastrous end.

We were still in the mountains and the hairpin bends were narrow and treacherous, with massive drops into oblivion. I felt uncomfortable driving at that speed, and Shorty's warnings were falling on deaf ears, but after our complete success in getting away with our ill-gotten gains, I felt indestructible.

Then it happened.

Negotiating a blind tight bend on a downhill run into one of the many valleys, I avoided a little rock fall. All through the mountain passes there were many roadside warnings, and plenty of visual evidence of recent falls.

I'm sure that had I driven through the small amount of rubble at a lower speed we would have been safe enough, but I had no time to think, and instinctively braked hard. What happened next was like a scene from of a slapstick movie.

The inertia on the roof rack, along with its contents, were too much, and the whole lot, completely intact, shot off the car's roof and headed on down the road at speed.

We looked at each other, both knowing that was the last we would see of our belongings, and that too after all the risks we took to get our souvenir.

We just sat there in our slowly moving car, following our out of control load to the next blind corner, knowing that in a very short space of time, and an even shorter length of road, our bits and pieces would be in the valley below.

Then a miracle happened. When we thought that all was lost, a small car with French licence plates came around the bend and up the hill. There wasn't much the approaching driver could do except to stop. He couldn't evade our projectile in the middle of the road, with a wall of crumbly cliff on one side and a sheer drop on the other.

The inevitable happened, and both moving objects gently came together like two long lost lovers.

The elderly French couple in the small car looked badly shaken, but apart from that it was a case of 'all's well that ends well'.

After we repositioned the luggage, we continued our journey, but were determined to stop for a beer and something to eat at the first opportune moment.

In a very short time we came upon a small but inviting village with several diners. We pulled into a car park adjacent to the café, and as soon as I got out of the car I heard a familiar voice shout out, "Hey Floyd."

We looked towards the entrance from where the shout had come from. There sitting outside was the American and English hikers who we had said our farewells to three days earlier. They had barely travelled any distance at all since they had left Llorett.

They were broke and starving, so we bought them breakfast and resumed our journey northwards, and said we would drop them off at Cologne.

It was good to be reunited with them, but we insisted that we would stop off for the night in Strasbourg. The intention was to have a night out on the town after finding a quiet place to park, but although it seemed a simple enough plan, it wasn't to be.

The first Guest House we tried refused us entry, and so did the next.

When we approached the next tavern, we were met at the entrance by burly doormen. Not only were we refused entry, but as before, it was always followed by a mouthful of abuse, and we realised that our American friend was causing the general unrest. He was the one people were pointing at when people were being vitriolic.

It dawned on us that it wasn't so much his hippy clothes, but the large Swastika he had on show. Eventually we managed to persuade him to tuck it into his T shirt. Even then we still faced many refusals before being allowed in anywhere for a drink. We realised that it was only when we moved into the German part of the city, away from the French district, that people accepted us as customers.

The next day we arrived in Cologne, and took them to their respective camps. We meant to have stayed in touch, but never did.

We were greeted like heroes when we presented our prize to our REME club. It certainly brightened the room up, and took pride of place behind the bar. It was only when we saw it hanging on the wall that made us appreciate its size and the risk we took to obtain it.

That first night back we celebrated to such an extent that I came close to drinking myself to death over a silly bet; again, I felt invincible. The Army has a long established drinking culture, and one of these is partaking in stupid bets involving alcohol. As I said, after our holiday I was on cloud 9 and felt indestructible, so was in a state of mind to take on any bet.

I was already three sheets to the wind when I took up the challenge to drink a pint of rum in half an hour. Yes, stupid is as stupid does!

I had a plan in my head to counter the smell of the rum, which I have always hated. My plan was to open my gullet and down as much as I could without stopping, hoping that I could at least get half of it down in one go. That would leave me about half a pint to sip or gulp in the remaining twenty-five minutes.

I never did know if I finished the bottle, because it was decided by the members in the club at that time to get me back to the barracks and put me to bed. They said it took three of them to carry me across the parade ground and into the barrack block.

Parts of what happened next I vaguely remember. As they were taking me down the corridor to mine and Shorty's room, a Corporal Green came out of the showers and into the corridor. He only had a white towel around his waist, which I think triggered a vision of sorts in my mind.

As we drew parallel with him, I broke away from my helpers, dived to the floor and grabbed his feet and ankles. At that moment in time I truly believed that I was Christ, and he was God, and I couldn't stop crying

Apparently, I was clawing on to his ankles so tightly that my helpers actually thought that they had broken a couple of my fingers trying to prise my grip from his feet.

It seems that a big discussion went on that night on whether they should phone for an ambulance or rush me to the medical centre. As I was out cold they let me sleep it off, but two watched over me that night.

I went to Corporal Green's room to apologise the next morning. He described his injuries to me, and promised to show me his feet and ankles once the bandages came off. Not a pretty sight!

Every day I would count my blessings about my posting to 50 Missile Regiment Minden, but after being there for just over a year, the Captain called me into the office. He informed me that they had just received notification of a new posting for me. It was in Germany still, but the large Infantry Workshop that I was being sent to would be relocated within a year back to Britain and become a part of the Catterick Garrison.

I had been so happy in this Shangri-la posting, but all good things come to an end, unfortunately. The CO asked me how I felt about it, and I told him how gutted I was, and how happy I was here.

"Right," he said. "That's what I thought. I'm not letting you go. Apart from fitting in from day one, you're the only Electrician we have."

He asked me to sit down, picked up the phone, and when he got connected he was soon screaming down the line, extolling my virtues. I had never seen him like that since the day I arrived, when he was trying to get rid of me. After a lengthy time, and during a pause in the argument he was having over the phone, he whispered to me to leave his office and that he would sort it.

As I was leaving, I heard him pleading the point that I had settled down and ended my disruptive ways, and whoever's decision it was must be mad to risk me reverting back to my old ways.

I waited for days to hear the outcome; none of it made any sense to me.

After a short while, I was summoned back to see Captain Fielding, who looked a broken man. He needn't have said anything. I knew he had failed in his attempt to keep me there.

I was given one week's leave before my posting to 12 Infantry Workshops stationed in Dortmund. It even crossed my mind that they had posted me to 50 Missile Regiment to serve under the Captain either as a punishment or to break my spirit.

My hatred for the Army and its uncompassionate ways rose to new heights, heights I never thought existed.

The opposite of signing in at a new posting was signing out of the posting that you are presently in. One of the unusual tasks I was given was to collect my medical records from the Medical centre, something I had never been asked to do before.

I couldn't resist steaming open the large envelope to take a peep, and what I found inside shook me rigid and filled me with a rage that I had never felt before. There inside was a printed form, separated by different sections with their own specialist headings. Headings such as 'Ambition'. Colonel Lawless had hand written, *'Smith's only Ambition is to get out of the Army.'* No argument there.

Another heading was 'Standing with Peers/Colleagues.' For this he had written, *'Smith suffers from extreme racial abuse by his peers, and cannot cope.'*

I believe this emanated from an incident which happened during my stay at Osnabruck. As far as I was concerned, I always looked back on it as one of the most humorous events in my Army career.

There was a certain soldier who slept in our 15 man barrack room. He couldn't help voicing supposedly witty remarks about my colour. The problem was never ending, morning, noon and night, every day for months. In fact it was every time he saw me. Most times his inane utterings were ignored, but it got to a point that no matter how many times I and my compadres warned him that he was being a bore, his onslaught continued. I was at the end of my patience. He just couldn't stop.

The inevitable happened and I snapped and dragged him behind our barracks. Suffice to say that he got the point. He went back to the barrack room bloodied and crying.

Racial tensions were riding high in the world at that time with the 'goings on' in America, concerning the Klu Klux Klan, and to some extent in Britain as well.

It soon got around that he had received his comeuppance.

That night just after lights out, our barrack room was unusually quiet, and you could cut the atmosphere with a knife. All of a sudden someone broke the silence, and because a number of us had a last fag before going to sleep, the cry went up, "Is something burning?" As quick as a flash the person I'd had the confrontation with earlier couldn't help himself, and through the darkness shouted out, "It's a fiery cross at the end of Eddie's bed."

The silence that followed was emphasised by the tension in the air, broken by my uncontrollable laughter. This whole episode became the camp joke.

Continuing reading my medical record, it was what was written under the heading of Family/Home Life that set my pulse racing and made me see red.

It said, "When Smith goes home, he assaults his elderly adopted mother."

This was a complete and infamous lie of mega proportions, and there was nothing that I could do about it. How could I admit to tampering with official post? He had written the report based on my SSAFA (Soldiers, Sailors, Air Force Association) representative back in my home town.

The name of the agent was included in the report.

I couldn't believe that he could make up such a story, but there again he was previously known as the Mad Major, and I didn't suppose that they get issued with a new brain, or charisma transplant when they get promoted.

Ironically, it was this report that eventually became the catalyst for my release from the Army a few years later. It was this very imaginative author who caused my father to have a stroke and eventually die.

A few years earlier my father refused to lie and help him get compensation for an industrial accident, which left the man partially crippled. This same man and his friends at the factory sent my father to 'Coventry', thus precipitating his stroke. I wasn't to find out this connection until I went home on my forthcoming leave.

Obviously I couldn't take the report from my medical files, as I wanted my mother to see it for herself. I had no doubt that she would not believe it unless she could read it with her own eyes.

There are a good many more stories I could tell about my time there.

I said goodbye to all my old friends, although we met up some months later when we all went to the Isle of Wight Music Festival.

# Chapter 9
## 5 Infantry Workshops

My story till now relates to the few years after leaving the Army, and looks back at all the good times as well as the bad times. More importantly, at the unbelievable times and situations that I found myself in.

From this time onwards is where the real, or some may say the unreal, story begins.

I will never be able to prove my story about my belief that I was shadowed by Her Majesty's Secret Service, but it's the only realistic solution to what happened next.

Just to recap on the silly, unfortunate incidents that happened over those past three years that may have made the powers that be have doubts about my dedication to my Army career, and more importantly my loyalty to the Crown.

First, I accidentally brought a large Army workshop to a standstill, which both the RAF and the rest of Allied forces had failed to do during the war.

I caused a part of a NATO military exercise to be halted because I got lost.

I was arrested and interrogated by the SIB (Special Investigation Branch) over the suspected arson of a military vehicle.

I was branded as the rebellious leader when the class revolted against retraining.

I was found guilty of desertion at a Courts Martial.

I joined and registered as a member of CND, in contravention of Army Regulation's, especially as I was about to be posted to a frontline missile regiment.

The previous events were bad enough, but they were mostly unintentional. What happened next 'was' intentional, but a bluff.

I took my one week's leave prior to my new posting to 5 Infantry Workshops, Dortmund. I had the intention of accepting the post, but only after going AWOL again.

I took my recently stolen medical records with me, and waited for the appropriate time to disclose its contents to my mother's side of the family

My mother came from a very large Victorian family, in fact she was one of 21 siblings. Although large, they were not a close family.

It happened to be a day that two of her closest sisters had come to visit, and I thought that would be the best time to produce my stolen report. At least they would become aware of how unfairly I had been treated, and why I was trying my hardest to force the Army to discharge me.

The effect was, as I expected, outrage and disbelief.

My mother, with the help of her sisters, decided to take joint action, and for the first time gave her the moral and practical support she needed. They contacted our MP again and also the church.

For my part I lied to the family about the length of leave I had been granted. Instead of the week I had been allotted, I told them I had two weeks.

I had decided that I would protest against the way I had been treated by deliberately missing my flight to Germany. This way they would have to reschedule my flight, which apart from making a protest, would give me an extra few days at home. I was expecting to be punished when I arrived there, but didn't care.

To make matters worse I took the one action that I knew the Army would not be able to tolerate.

I sent a declaration of war to the Ministry of Defence, stating my name, rank and number.

To make sure that I would get as much publicity as possible, I copied my declaration by writing out four seperate copies, and sending one to each of the main daily newspapers of the day: *The Mirror*, *The Mail*, *The Daily Express* and a fore runner of the *Sun*, the *Daily Sketch*.

Obviously I never would dream of taking such a course of action, I just wanted to get under the skin of the top brass. It seemed like a good idea at the time.

They sent me fresh travel tickets via the local Police, and nothing else was ever said about my AWOL. They just accepted my ready-made excuse.

Not at anytime was the matter of my war declaration ever mentioned or brought up, from that day to this. I would imagine in this day and age, had I employed the same course of tactics, I would be immediately incarcerated and the key thrown away.

The only response was a very short and curt letter from the Daily Mail telling me not to be so stupid.

Nothing was said when I arrived at 5 Infantry in Dortmund. I just collected my bedding etc. and booked in as normal. Talk about weird!

An unfortunate incident happened on that first day, after booking in which nearly landed me in jail.

I was told to take the rest of the day off, and report for duty the next morning, so I thought that I would take myself out of camp and go downtown to Dortmund to get a feel for the place.

Just outside the main gate of the camp was a tram stop. I had never been on these bendy flexible trams before, so it was a small adventure for me.

The tram was only half full, but as we got closer to the City centre it began to fill up rapidly, and it didn't take long before all the seats were taken.

With the main shopping centre in sight the tram jerked to a halt at the next stop, and a large group of passengers boarded. At the front of the crowd was an elderly lady who seemed to have a lot of trouble trying to balance her walking stick on her arm whilst putting her purse away in her handbag. Her one hand was firmly holding on to the back of the seats as she progressed down the aisle.

What happened next was absolute mayhem.

As she approached me, four things happened simultaneously. I stood up to offer my seat. She dropped her purse as the tram started off with a jerk. I bent down to retrieve it, so did she, and our heads collided. She was propelled backwards into the line of travellers, and I was left holding her purse. Before I could react in anyway at all, a group of passengers jumped on me. During the chaos I heard the word Police mentioned, and a row broke out amongst various Germans. Although I was being firmly held down, I did get a glimpse of the elderly lady being helped up, and I realised that some of the travellers thought that I was trying to rob her. She looked slightly concussed, but managed to smile and calm the situation down. All I could do was apologise as best as I could and get off the tram at the next stop. I never did get to see Dortmund that day, and headed back to camp.

The next morning I reported to the Electrical Engineers department. I was the only Electrician, amongst five or six Electronic engineers, all NCOs, with a Staff Sergeant in charge.

This is where I first came face to face with who I now believe was the first of four of my suspected government shadows. I would point out, that looking back, even though all four were different in many aspects they all had the same overriding basic traits.

Firstly, no matter what group of friends I associated with, I was their only friend, and however hard I tried to include them into my group of peers, they all seemed very offish and reluctant to make ties with anyone else.

Secondly, and most important, they had a quiet strength about them. No one would ever cross swords with them, no matter how big and macho that person might be.

Thirdly, and this sounds silly, their appearance was always clean cut and immaculate. Too immaculate!

Lastly, they lived and played by their own rules, and regulations never seemed to get in their way.

I will give them all assumed names, as if I am right in my suspicions then they may still be active today.

On my first day of duty I was introduced to the first of my four shadows. We will call him Paul Longham. He was a Lance Corporal and his trade was in electronics. He immediately made me welcome. I soon realised that he seemed ill at ease with everyone else around him.

A few weeks later my peers explained why they felt disgruntled. He seemed to get away with the normal everyday duties and mundane roles that everyone else were required to do. I saw no evidence of this initially, but a few months later I realised exactly what people meant.

The general consensus amongst my colleagues was that Paul's father was a very high ranking officer working out of the Ministry of Defence in London.

It seemed logical and no one, especially me, doubted the fact. He certainly was treated with respect, almost reverence by Senior NCOs and commissioned officers.

We spent a lot of our spare time together visiting the lively bars, including the out of bound bars which were situated downtown in the Red Light district of Dortmund.

Very occasionally there would be a group of us out on the town, but more times than not these nights ended acrimoniously in arguments, nearly always about politics.

It's important to mention this at this stage that I, like a good many others, chose to voice my points of view after a few beers on almost any subject except politics. It used to bore me to tears as I knew very little about the subject, and at that time never wanted to. That change came some time later. Paul just never knew when to stop. Consequently it was mostly the two of us who painted the town red.

There was one exception, which really stands out. It happened to be Paul's birthday on this particular weekend in question, and he wanted to start off at a disco on the outskirts of town, which was difficult to get to on the public transport system. So he borrowed a car from somebody for the night, and off we set, Paul, myself and four others cramped into this old banger.

It was winter time, the roads were very icy because of the extreme cold, but thankfully no snow.

In fact, the venue we ended up at was as good as Paul said it would be, the only little white lie he told was its location. It wasn't on the outskirts, but was in the next town, a good few miles away.

Time passed by so quickly, that before we knew it the place shut down and it was 3 in the morning. As was expected Paul was wasted; in fact we all were.

Unlike nowadays, mobiles hadn't been invented. We considered trying to get back into the night club, to ask them to phone a taxi for us, but we soon dismissed the idea as it was hard enough for us to speak the Queen's English in the state we were in, let alone trying to use the limited German phrases we knew.

In any case Paul had promised to return the car that morning.

A couple of the group were insistent on driving, one of them unable to stand unaided. Paul would have none of it and said that I was the only one he had faith in.

His confidence in me sobered me up a touch; it was either that or the fear I was feeling right then. We squeezed into the car, three in front and three in the back. It was a bitterly cold foggy night, which was to cause our first major problem. After managing to get the car started and locating the light switch we set off.

The windscreen was thick with ice, and had we any wits about us we would have insured that the wipers weren't firmly stuck. Unfortunately, when they were switched on, the ominous bang followed by the burning smell told its own story, that the wiper motor was blown. The heater switch must have been on the same circuit, and that wouldn't work either.

Someone had the bright idea of relieving ourselves on the windscreen to defrost it.

It was a work of art just to keep our balance on the slippery bonnet, but eventually we had all emptied our bladders. The outcome had the opposite effect we had hoped for: instead of getting rid of the ice, we had only made the ice thicker and completely non transparent.

We all agreed that our only way of keeping warm that night was to huddle together and hope that we survived till morning.

We had only just settled down for the night when somebody came up with another brainwave. He had noticed that the car had a sunroof. Before he could say what was on his mind, my brain was thinking of arguments against it.

The idea was, as we were all geared up in our warm parkas, I was to drive, and the other five were to take it in turns to navigate with their heads protruding through the sunroof, and to shout down directions and warnings. I quickly pointed out that our camp was on the other side of Dortmund, besides which, the chances of being picked up by the police were very high, and me being the driver it would be my neck on the block. Everyone agreed that if the police became involved, we would all admit to being the driver. Then the third crazy idea of the night was suggested. We were close to the Autobahn, as was the camp, and at that time in the morning it would be quiet, with less turns and no traffic lights,

So off we set at a very steady pace, with everyone's adrenalin pumping. We made better than expected progress, nearly hitting a few trees and road signs, but all in all we were in good spirits, especially as we had found a half bottle of scotch in the glove box.

It was bitterly cold for the person who was the watcher and whose head was protruding from the sun roof. It seemed an age trying to reach the motorway, although in truth it only took about half an hour. I found that my main problem was that the longer we continued without incident, the more confident I was becoming. My passengers were very vocal at the speed that we were travelling, and begged me to slow down.

Suddenly a cry went up that the motorway lights were in sight; we all felt that the worst was over. How wrong could we be!

By the time we turned on to the motorway, the fog had thickened into a real 'pea souper'. We guessed that it was only about ten miles before we needed to exit, and then only a very short road to the camp. We had only been travelling for about five minutes when our lookout screamed that we were on a collision course with an oncoming car. Shock! Horror! We were travelling up the Autobahn on the wrong side. Not being able to see, my mind froze, which we realised afterwards probably saved our lives. Had I been a bit more compos mentis, then I'm sure I would have taken an evasive action of some sort, which could have been disastrous.

We now had to make a decision: should we carry on or turn around.

By our reckoning we had travelled so far and only met one vehicle coming our way, so we all believed that as far as it went luck was on our side. The thick fog was as big an aide to us as it was a problem, and so we carried on.

The next few miles seemed to take a lifetime, and I was secretly thanking God that I was still alive. I never knew it then, but the nearest that I have ever been to death was about ten minutes away, just when I thought the worst was over.

As I said, on my first day at 5 Infantry Workshops, I caught a tram downtown from the stop just outside of the camp's main gate.

The two tram lines ran in between the dual carriageway.

The carriageway that we were approaching the camp on was significantly lower than the tram tracks that we needed to cross. This meant there was a substantial slope to get up before we could cross the tracks, then a further slope to reach our camp gates.

We all agreed that we would need to succeed the first time, and as the roads were dangerously icy, we needed to make the turn at the right time and with enough speed to mount the slope. This would take some doing.

To make the car lighter, four got out and walked to the start of the incline. They would then be on hand, just in case there was not enough traction on the ice to make it to the top. Luckily there were no other vehicles around when we started our approach. Just me and the guiding watcher in the sun roof, whose main concern was to let me know when to turn, and also to gauge my speed on the ice.

It was a mixture of alcohol and bravado which gave me the courage to attempt it. Anyway, no turning back now, I just had to put my trust in the watcher and concentrate.

I went as fast as I dared so that the car wouldn't skid when I turned. My watcher shouted instructions. I gently swung the wheel, and as soon as I felt the vehicle straighten up, I felt the ramp and accelerated. The instant relief swept over me when I felt my front wheels make contact with the first set of rails. This caused the car to stall, and at the same time the whole world lit up with a massive blue flash, followed swiftly by alternating yellow and black stripes. Initially I thought it was an explosion, but of course it was an early tram coming out of the mist heading into town to start its day.

Despite Paul being drunk he realised the danger. We had missed the downtown tram but were straddled across the uptown track. He ran to the guardhouse and came back within minutes with a group of men on guard duty, even those that had been asleep.

Our six plus the others made short work in pushing the car in to the camp and to safety.

Now, normally any incident would be recorded in the Incident Book for security reasons, especially one as big as this, as it involved most of the Guard. It would have, or should have at least been investigated, but none of us ever heard anything about the events of that night. Rumour was that Paul had used his powers of persuasion once again. We will never know.

The next incident concerning Paul's influence in the Army was the talk of the camp and really set tongues wagging.

It was just a normal day at work, and what happened was even more surprising as our camp was virtually a closed unit except for a handful of civilians that were employed there. In fact out of all the camps I had been to this was the most security conscious of them all.

Just before the lunch time break, Paul took me to one side and explained that he had obtained permission from the CO to allow his brother to meet up with him in the canteen during our meal. Apparently, his brother was hitch hiking back to Britain from the Far East.

So off he went about twenty minutes before the rest of us for his meal.

I, like everyone else, was more than interested in knowing what he looked like, and if he came across as anti-social as his brother.

When we arrived at the canteen it was pretty well full, except for a corner which was reserved for senior NCOs.

At this time, the only people sitting there were Paul and a scruffy looking hippy with a bushy beard and a very colourful caftan. They were engrossed in discussion, but although there were a couple of Military Police standing near to them, we assumed it was because his brother was non MOD. I still believed that after they finished their chat, Paul would bring his 'brother' over to introduce him to us, especially me, his best mate. It never happened, so we were never to find out if he had as strong a Glaswegian accent as Paul.

There were many incidents I had with Paul on a night out in which I thought we had a guardian angel looking after us. One of the most serious ones happened out of the blue at the end of a particularly uneventful night.

As usual he was pretty well wasted with drink, but was in a happy mood, as he had found no one to argue politics with. We stopped at the German equivalent of a Fish & Chip shop, and ordered what we wanted. The shop was quite full, being the end of the night. The rage Paul went into was so unexpected and so violent, it took me, the shop owner and customers by surprise. Whether his meal was cold, had too much salt, or if he was short changed I never knew. He threw his meal at the owner, but before anyone, including me, could react, he started throwing bottles and anything else he could find. In about two minutes it looked like a bomb had exploded.

I managed to drag him out whilst the owner was on the phone to the police. I feared the worst. I knew the Police would be waiting for us back at the camp. Paul had settled down as quickly as he flared up. We booked back into camp as normal then, and the incident was never referred to again.

Dortmund was a great city to let your hair down in and we had some great nights out.

I will always remember one drinking session we had, in The Hole in the Wall guest house. This establishment stayed open 24/7, and was in the centre of the red light district. Its main aim was to give shelter and nourishment to the local prostitutes who were on a break, but it had its fair share of working women, who for the want of a better phrase, were past their sell by date. They relieved certain patrons whilst sitting at the many tables, some of which were in stalls.

We came to this pub whenever we wanted a good time as they always had good groups on, many of whom were English. Plenty of girls, cheap drink and good music, what else could a man ask for.

One Easter there was half a dozen of us started off to the *Hole* to begin our boozy night out pub crawling as usual, but someone suggested a quick game of cards. This turned into a marathon with at least one of us at different times flaking out in a drunken stupor and then recovering to carry on playing. We started the game early on Good Friday night, and finally wound up the drinking and the game Easter Monday afternoon.

There's another reason that I will never forget the The Hole in the Wall as it affected my life ever since.

On the nights that they had music on, they employed doormen, but the chief bouncer was a woman. She was built like a brick shithouse, about six three, with tall short blonde hair and an ugly scar across her face. You wouldn't want to cross her, and none of us ever did.

This one particular night, quite late, there was a commotion at the door. Nothing unusual there, but the brawl found its way into the pub.

The lady bouncer grabbed the nearest thing to her to use as a weapon. Unfortunately, it was the chair that I was sitting on. I had been sitting with my back to the door, and next thing I knew I was sprawled on the ground and found myself looking up at the bunch of protagonists fighting above me. I had had a few unintended boots to the head. I couldn't get up, I just curled up into a ball and tried to protect my head.

Afterwards, she apologised once she regained control, but from that day to this I have a phobia about sitting with my back to a crowd, that includes buses, restaurants and the like.

My time in Dortmund was soon to come to an end, but it's a city I loved and truly missed.

# Chapter 10
## Catterick Garrison

I knew when my posting came through to 5 Infantry that the Unit was to be reallocated back to England in the near future. This came sooner than expected, and all leave was cancelled, as it would need everybody to pull their weight to make the transition smooth. Everything had to be packed and stored away, all in a weekend.

Of course there was one absentee from these proceedings, which never came as much of a surprise to anyone, and that absentee was Paul. Somehow he had been granted leave for the duration of the move. I, like everyone else, firmly believed that it was the status and influence of Paul's father that gave him these special privileges.

The unit was mobilised and left Dortmund in the early hours of Monday morning. The route which we took was to travel north to one of the major ports in northern Germany, then by ship across the North Sea to the North East of England.

The final destination was to the Catterick garrison, which was going to be the workshops' new home.

The transportation of the many trucks and equipment went smoothly, and because of the large number of the advanced group of soldiers which had gone on ahead to prepare for the huge convoy's arrival, we all knew that once we had arrived that the next morning we could start our one week's leave, the advance group having had theirs before we arrived.

That night, having met up again with Paul, we hit all the pubs in the little town of Richmond, some more than once. I did confide to Paul that I had no intention of coming back after my leave, and would go sick for a week, just to show the Army that

I was still a law unto myself. I felt that they owed me that much.

So after my first week's holiday I phoned the camp up from a phone box and told them I wasn't fit to travel. The person at the other end of the line seemed agitated and angry, and started quoting Queen's Regulations to me, but after listening for a minute or so, I hung up.

On my return, as expected, I was marched in front of my commanding officer to receive my punishment. This turned out to be two weeks in the Glass House, but the powers that be had a very nasty trick up their sleeve.

Before they took me to the guard room to begin my ordeal, they escorted me to the medical centre, which I didn't consider that unusual, but boy, was I in for a shock! I was taken into a small room, and told to strip naked; nothing unusual with that, as this is what they did at Colchester. The only difference being that normally you strip as a group and stand in a line, and told to cough when someone holds your crown jewels.

This time I was on my own, and once stripped, my escorts told me to turn around.

It was only then that I realised that there was another door in the room, opposite the one in which we had entered.

One escort opened the door whilst the other one pushed me forward into a very large room, which was really more of a hall.

What happened next was so traumatic that I can't remember what was said or what occurred. All I remember was that I found myself in front of tables set out in a very large U shape. There were about ten student nurses sitting on each side to my left and right, and on the top table sat a mixture of men and women, who I assumed were student doctors.

I have no recollection of how long I was subjected to this humiliation, or the reason why. In fact I'm glad that my memory blanked out any of the details, otherwise I may have been mentally scarred for life.

I was returned half a mile up the road to the guardroom by the escort, where I found myself sharing a cell with three other soldiers from the nearby Armoured Regiment.

One of these was a highly charismatic soldier called Bobby Wenton, who was as much an exhibitionist as Bob Carlisle from Bradford. Bobby came from Liverpool, and like me, was a half caste. He seemed to have soul music coursing through his veins, and never stopped performing songs from The Four Tops & Temptations. He created such an impression on me in those two short weeks of my term of incarceration. I must assume that it was mutual, as by the end of my sentence he had tried every which way to set me up with his sister Anna back in Liverpool. He saw me as his future brother in law.

His big dream was to have his own Soul group, and to enter on to the stage to the song of Sam & Dave's 'Soul Man'. I always wondered if he ever made it; he certainly had the talent and charisma.

The reason I tell this very important story is because I feel that those two weeks with Bobby helped me to forget the trials and tribulations of the medical centre. I felt I owed him big time.

On returning to the REME workshop, I was surprised to see how much man power had been added to the workforce, and even more surprised to find that Paul had been given an extended leave, and did not return until two weeks later.

This was very opportune for me as one of the newcomers in our technical section was a Lance Corporal, who became one of the closest friends that I ever had. Trevor Dalton. I feel that had Paul been there, then a very special bond would not have been formed between us.

The biggest surprise of all for me on my return to our section was the way that I was treated, especially by the senior ranks. It was almost as if people had been told to take it very easy on me, and treat me with kid gloves.

Trevor was newly married, and he and his new young bride Brenda never applied for married quarters. Instead they rented a private flat in the nearby town of Richmond. The view was incredible, as it looked directly down a steep valley on to the river Swale.

Brenda never really moved into their flat due to the fact that all was not well medically with her family, so she lived in her family home at Bracknell.

Trevor being the great friend that he was, allowed me the use of their flat for the weekends, which allowed Paul and myself a convenient base to explore the many pubs in the vicinity.

In those days, the popular genre of music was the protest song, such as Zager & Evans big hit 'In the Year 2525'.

Trevor was fairly competent on the guitar, and I could throw the odd lyric together, so he suggested that we should try and break into the music business. We wrote under the name of Chaz & Devine, and even to this day neither one of us could remember who was 'Chaz' and who was 'Devine'. Most of our attempts were at best futile, but one, which we called 'Eighth Days Noon's Day' was so good that after several failed attempts to contact one of the times leading music impresario's, Mickey Most, (Trevor had found out where his London residence was), and camped on his front lawn. He never got to see him, just managed to get arrested.

The Catterick garrison was basically a small town, with different regiments and units scattered here and there, so you needed transport to get around. Trevor was surprised that no one except for me could seem to use the little one ton truck, which was allotted to our unit as a utility vehicle. One day Trevor rumbled me. He realised that I had installed a secret switch into the ignition system, which left it disabled to anyone else who wanted to it for their personal use.

There were notice boards scattered around the town, outside the entrance to the various Companies, keeping all informed about future events for individual units, and more importantly for the garrison in general. I found these very informative.

One day I was shocked to find that a NATO exercise was planned in Norway, during the winter months. Most would have found this exciting, but I didn't do cold! So I kept a close watch on our notice board. One of the very many bits of information which jumped out at me, was the phrase, 'A skeleton force is to be left behind to look after the camp, and should anyone have a personal reason why they should remain behind, then they should submit their reasons, before a set date, to their Company Commander. Should there not be enough volunteers, then a ballot would be held.'

It worked in Bordon, so why not here? As soon as I saw the notice go up, I took it down, then submitted my letter to relieve myself of the Norway fiasco. I never told anyone, not even Trevor, which made me feel bad. I waited until I had confirmation, which was about a week before the closing date, then I showed the missive to Trevor. He wasn't too pleased at first, in fact he was as angry as I had ever known.

All's well that ends well! He had enough time to plan a good enough excuse, to get his letter in, and get confirmation of his release to stay behind. Of course I put the notice back up on the relevant notice boards, giving others a chance. I never felt guilty for not letting Paul in on it, as I knew he could swing it had he wanted to. He always did.

The day arrived for the camp to empty, and we were a party of ten, left with instructions to keep us busy for the two weeks whilst the company were abroad, painting and such like.

There was no shirking. We all got stuck into the tasks set for us, as we all agreed that the sooner we had finished, then the sooner we could relax and enjoy our newly found free time.

Working hard we were pleased to find that our maintenance jobs were all finished in a matter of a few days. This however left us with a lot of dead time on our hands, so we racked our brains, trying to think of ways to amuse ourselves. Each one of us had come up with ideas, which we tried, but it was my idea which won the day.

One of our duties, whilst the main body of men were away on exercise, was to make sure that the workshops were secure, along with the large amount of soldiers' cars left behind during the time that everyone was away.

This meant that about forty to fifty cars were garaged in the very large main workshop. For safety reasons all cars had to be left unlocked, with their keys left in the ignition. This was in case of emergencies such as a fire. Then all the vehicles could be moved to safety outside.

In those days most gear sticks featured small round knobs with an embossed picture of the gear sequence on the top.

My brainwave was to unscrew the gear knobs to use as golf balls, then using lengths of rubber and steel pipes laid on the floor to act as putting holes.

This worked really well, but our big failing was that we had unscrewed more knobs than we needed, to try out which ones suited best for our makeshift course. We used pickaxe handles from the stores to act as putters.

Nearing the end of our two week activities, someone casually mentioned that it would be funny if we hadn't kept a check on which knob belonged to which car. This casual remark hit us all like a cannon ball, and panic set in. A good percentage of the cars in the workshop belonged to officers and non-commissioned officers, which made our predicament more worrying.

Luckily for us they had decided to leave our utility vehicle behind, and not take it to Norway, as it seemed unreliable. So for the next few days we toured the area, checking the local garages and cross referencing the gear knobs of the vehicles to the cars in our care. We were well pleased when we managed to match each one with the correct vehicle.

I never realised it then, but my time serving in the British Army was soon coming to an end, but there was one very significant event that happened, which was really unexpected and out of this world.

As I have already said, Paul had never been treated like a regular soldier, and always with reverence and awe, and since I had returned from my absence I was granted certain favours, but what was about to happen shook even me.

The Regiments and Companies in the Northern region of England held a biannual cross country motor rally. This was a very exclusive and prestigious event. Each of the Regiments were allowed two teams to represent them.

A team was usually made up of a driver and one navigator, consisting of a commissioned officer and a senior non-commissioned officer. It was deemed to be a great honour to be picked from the many eager senior ranks who had put their names forward.

Out of the blue Paul casually asked me one day if I fancied it; of course I said yes, but I knew it was just wishful thinking on his part.

Next day he told me that we were one of the two teams to represent the regiment. I couldn't believe it! I couldn't believe how he could have possibly fixed it, but when it came to Paul anything was possible. It was obvious that a lot of people, mainly officers, resented it, and in the forthcoming weeks it certainly made me feel uncomfortable.

Come the day of the rally, I was so excited and determined to do well, but the only word to sum up the experience was, farcical, with a capital F.

Picture the scene. About a hundred Land Rovers, each with two men all geared up and filled with excitement, engines running, drivers hunched over their steering wheels, navigators studying their maps, compasses at the ready.

We were team forty something, and that was our starting position, each team leaving at two minute intervals. I had told Paul, that as soon as we left the Camp gates, which was the starting line, to turn right.

The green flag went up, the whistle was blown and the first team went out of the gate, and turned left. Paul and I were falling about laughing at the mistake they had made, and again when the second team followed suit; we could hardly contain ourselves. Each team turned left, and when the twenty odd one did the same, Paul started doubting my navigational skills, and quickly checked the map and clues, but came up with the same directions as I did.

He was always self-assured, which surprised me all the more when he said, "I'm convinced it's a right turn out of the gate, but I'm turning left, I don't want to look a fool."

I managed to make him think again that maybe we were right and all previous teams were wrong, or perhaps it's a test and half the competitors are meant to go the other way.

No, he was determined to follow the rest, even though it was against his better nature.

Up to the gates he went. I told him how disappointed I was, as I thought he had more faith in me. Through the gates he went, and turned right!

As I said it was a cross country rally, and by our calculations half a mile down the road, we were due to go off road and into the countryside. So we decided to hide our jeep in amongst the trees, and satisfy ourselves by watching the other competitors go by.

Unfortunately, it wasn't to be. We were gutted!

The problem now was to get back on the right trail, but if we were caught on a road by the many stewards, then we would be instantly disqualified. There was only one option left, without losing face, and that was to assume that we actually did turn right at the gates and try and pick up the correct course.

Paul had spread the map out on the flat bonnet of the jeep, and put the binoculars, compass and the plastic see through protractors on top of the map for us to study a way out of our predicament. I had said that I was going into the trees to relieve myself before we put our heads together.

As I emerged from the trees, I saw Paul pick up the binoculars and turn away towards the valley laid out below us, and was busily scanning the countryside for our competitors' vehicles. Thing was, the implements on the map had been put there to secure it in the moderate wind, which was prevalent at the time.

Just as I approached the jeep, the wind picked up quickly, and a massive gust lifted the map, the heavy compass sliding off the bonnet and falling to the ground. The map with the light weight protractors soared up in the air, and after a lot of swirling about ended up in the uppermost branches of a young tall tree. It sat there like a flag, taunting us. We had not seen the protractors fall off, they could have been anywhere. We searched the undergrowth, but because of their transparency we had no hope of finding them, unless we had some idea where to start looking. Without them the map would be useless.

Not wanting to give up, all that we could do was to travel the countryside, avoiding the roads in the hope of catching sight of any of the rally vehicles. It was futile, so we gave up. Not wanting to go back, we spent the rest of the day in a café near Scotch Corner.

Once we got back, Paul told me not to worry, he would sort it. I presumed that he did, as I never heard any more and there was no negative comeback.

I was discharged from the Army within a month of the rally fiasco. How it came about surprised even me, especially the speed of it after four long years of waiting. What brought my victory about is only supposition on my part, and I can only record the events.

Some weeks before, my mother had written to the Queen asking for my release from Army service. Had my mother's hand writing been more legible, then what happened next might have had a different outcome.

The reply swiftly came back to my mother from Buckingham Palace, informing her that her request had been forwarded to the Home Office. Just as quickly, she had a reply from the Home Office, asking various questions, such as '*What prison is your son in?*' '*What was his offence?*' '*How long was his sentence?*' '*When is he due to release?*' and so on.

Mother swiftly wrote back, stating that I wasn't in prison, but in the Army, and that she wanted me out.

The speed of the reply was outstanding, just a brief letter saying that the case had been forwarded to the Ministry of Defence.

A week later I was ordered in front of my commanding officer, who informed me that I had won my case, and that the price of discharge would be £200, which was the going rate for an 'A Class' engineer. So my fight to buy myself out was finally over.

One small thing stood in my way. I had no money!

I was granted a few days leave to try and sort out a loan.

Characteristically, Trevor jumped in and said that he and his new bride had just over £200 in their bank, and he wrote a letter of intent for me to offer as security to any bank that would furnish me the money as a loan.

After approaching three banks, I realised it was hopeless, as after their laughter subsided, they all virtually said the same. Instead of using Trevor's money as security, ask him for the loan. I had no doubt that if I had asked him, he would have done so, even if it was reluctantly.

I decided not to, as I thought that the idea of a young bride seeing her hard earned money being given to a complete stranger was unacceptable. There was nothing for it but to go back to camp and tell my CO and Trevor that I couldn't raise the money.

The CO told me to go back and carry on my duties, and he would see what he could do. This was Monday, December 15th.

There are two relevant parts to this story. Firstly, I was down to replace my NATO identity card on the Wednesday. Secondly, my immediate duties were to sort out the Christmas lights in the Canteen, which we shared with civilians employed in our camp. I had painted them a variety of colours, and was waiting for them to dry, with the intention of writing a Christmas message in white, with one letter on each bulb,

Tuesday morning came, and the first thing that happened was that I was issued with my new NATO card, and told to take my old one to the Admin office before dinner. Before I had chance to, I was informed that the Adjutant wanted to see me. So off I went to the main block.

I was informed, "They've decided to release you without the £200 payment, so today is your last day, finish up what you are doing, because you must be off the camp by Wednesday dinnertime."

This was a shock to the system, as I quickly realised that I had no money to pay for my travel home. I begged him to postpone my leaving until the Thursday, which was payday. He was deaf to my pleas. I was gutted, but good old Trevor stepped up to the mark, and gave me the money, knowing he might never get it back. He did eventually, but what a mate!

All that was left was for me to vent my anger and try to give the Army something to remember me by.

As I have said, my duty at that moment was to prepare the Christmas lights in the canteen ready for the Christmas dinner and dance on the forthcoming Friday night, before the regiment broke up for the Winter recess.

My plan to get revenge on the military establishment was admittedly immature, but gave me a lot of pleasure. It would be my last passing shot at the Army.

The last day before discharge, my job was to get the Christmas lights painted. I thought up the longest message possible, but made sure that the colours were not in sequence. There were literally scores of bulbs in half a dozen different shades, and the message as far as I can remember went: '*A VERY MERRY CHRISTMAS AND A HAPPY NEW YEAR TO ALL THE TROOPS AND CIVILIAN EMPLOYEES OF 5 INFANTRY WORKSHOP CATTERICK.*'

I then mixed them up and carefully placed them in a box to dry, and went off to pack. This, although a childish prank, gave me satisfaction and comfort for many years to come.

On my last day, I said goodbye to Trevor and Paul. We swapped addresses and vowed to stay in touch, but I never believed that we would. In fact, mine and Trevor's friendship grew and we never lost touch; he was always there for me in the wanderlust years that were to follow. He went on to write a good many horror books, my favourite being *Open Tap,* which one day I am sure will make it onto the silver screen.

Now, Paul was a different kettle of fish. I never expected to hear from him for some time, but it was within a month that I received a letter from him saying that he was allowed to buy himself out of Army service. Now when you think how long it had taken me because of my trade qualifications, and here was Paul, not only a NCO, but a X class tradesman in electronics, who seemed to have unlimited influence.

He asked me if I would meet him in Liverpool on a set day, as he was travelling from Glasgow to attend a job interview in the city. If he was successful then he would be working in Newcastle. We arranged to meet at Lime Street station in the afternoon, after his interview.

I don't remember much because, as usual, we ended quite blotto after a very short time.

The one incident that I do remember was after a series of pubs, with Paul trying to start political arguments in each one. I was getting really fed up.

Out of boredom, I was standing at the bar looking around for something to occupy my time, as I found political debates very tedious.

I spotted a dog sitting by a corner table just staring at me; he was with a group of elderly people, and one man held the leash he was attached to. He was remarkable, his eyes never left mine. At this point none of the people at the table or in the bar had noticed our staring competition, until I upped the ante and started showing my teeth. The dog responded with a series of growls, which drew attention to what was going on. The more animated I became the more agitated he became. Shouts of "leave him alone!" were ringing out, but I couldn't stop, I don't know what came over me.

Next thing I knew, I had taken off my jacket, and was tormenting the dog by using it like a matadors' cape. By this time the dog was straining at the leash to get at me. I shall never know why I didn't stop, it was way out of character for me.

All of a sudden, a chorus of shouts went up of, "let him off the leash, Harry!"

And he did. He went for my coat, and in a matter of minutes it was ripped to shreds. I don't remember much after that, except being in a taxi and arriving at the train station. Paul got out, I thought to pay the fare. Instead he shouted "run!" which I did. Next minute I was on the train heading to Birmingham.

I never saw Paul again, but about a month later he sent me a small cardboard box containing some wedding cake, with the simple message, '*All the best for the future.*'

It was many years later that I came to believe that he was the first of at least four people that had entered my life, who I am sure belonged to the Security Service.

A pattern was to emerge, that as one left, another soon took their place, and then departed my life as quickly as they came.

# Chapter 11
## The End of Home Life

After I had been given a compassionate discharge out of the Army where I served as a Vehicle Electrician from 1964 to 1969, I soon found a job as a stop gap to give me breathing space while deciding what to do with my life.

I took a job as a labourer in Terry's (the spring makers) Warehouse. There, I met the second person who I now believe to have been a shadow. With my previous history, such as declaring war on the Army, the government would be pretty remiss if this action wasn't forthcoming. In fact, in the next few years, I reckon I could add at least another two companions to that list.

I made a lot of friends once I got back to my home town of Redditch, but one person in particular was Don Abbot, a barman from Plymouth who was employed in one of the hot spots for young people called the Unicorn.

We became very close, like brothers, and were to enjoy many escapades together. Another person I became close to was Brendan Maguire, and the three of us became great party goers. A lot of my old friends had married or moved on whilst I was serving my time in the Army, so it was great having a circle of friends again without the possibility of a posting interrupting comradeships.

At this point, I should tell you how and where I met my travelling partners.

Within a week of working in the factory, I was introduced to a well dressed new employee who had just been taken on to work in the warehouse where I was employed, and although not working alongside me, as he had a different job, he was in close proximity to my place of work. We immediately became close friends and were soon spending most of our leisure time together.

His name was Eugene and he came from Belfast, Northern Ireland. Looking back over the years, I have been more and more convinced that he worked for the British Intelligence Services.

Eugene was a legend in his own lifetime. I have never in my life met any man who could pull women like he could, in fact he never had to try. It was mainly due to his good looks. The only way to describe him was that he was a doppelganger to the most famous of all Irish footballers of that time, George Best. He came from the same area as George did, with the same smile and Irish twang. He was so alike to the footballer that no one would believe him when he said he wasn't related. It became so boring to him that it was easier to say he was George's cousin, and people believed it. He found it so easy to pick up women that the thrill of the chase was no longer there. Instead, he concentrated on 'Hen Nights', not because of the abundance of women, rather his prey was always the intended bride to be. He made it look all too simple, and his strike rate was well over the 50% mark.

We went everywhere together, and had some great times. I especially enjoyed our odd nights out in the Digbeth area of Birmingham, which is where there is a well-known Irish club and numerous Irish bars. With my love for Irish music, I couldn't get enough of it, but it being a twenty-five-mile round trip we were lucky to get there on a monthly basis. I was surprised how many people, both men and women, knew Eugene. I assumed that he had lived in Birmingham before I knew him.

I have said how successful he was with the opposite sex, but one incident really unnerved me.

In my home town of Redditch, with its large contingency of West Indian immigrants, Reggae was very popular, well before it became a huge hit in Britain. A Reggae dance was held once a month in the Royal Hotel. Whole families would attend, from small children to the aged.

There was one occasion where Eugene spent the night on the dance floor with a strikingly attractive girl. It was obvious that they fancied each other, and our group knew that he had scored again. It surprised everyone that once the dancing was finished Eugene came back to the group and made no attempt to leave with her and claim the spoils of his chase.

So I asked him what was up, as I thought he would have at least taken her home. His reply really shook me when he said, "No problem, I'm meeting up with her later at her house."

"Why not walk her home?" I asked.

"Because she's coloured and I don't want to be seen walking through the town with her," he said.

I pointed out that me and him went everywhere together and that she was as lightly coloured as I was, maybe even lighter. He just shrugged and left it at that.

One night when we were out, he said he had to meet up with friends from Ireland who had come over for a short break and wanted to meet me so that they could put a face to a name.

We met in the Plough and Harrow lounge, as arranged by Eugene. There were three of them, two young men and a particularly pretty young girl, all from Belfast. One of them was introduced as Seamus who was Eugene's life-long best friend, the other pair were engaged. All three were only staying for the night, and then moving on to Birmingham first thing the next morning.

Eugene was great company to be with, but his only fault was that he was for ever trying to persuade me to go to Jersey in the Channel Islands. As much as I was tempted, I felt that I couldn't consider the move because of my mother. I owed her so much, and besides, I had been offered employment for two jobs with good money and a promising future, either working for the *Midland Red* bus company in Birmingham as a qualified electrician, or as a semi-skilled mechanic working at the local depot in my home town.

It seemed that for once I had something to look forward to, with no foreseen problems and a future with prospects.

I should only be so lucky!

You would think that in my short life I would have already had my fair share of upsets, disappointments and traumas, but what was about to happen changed everything.

I hadn't told my mother about the job prospects until I had made up my mind which offer to take. I will never forget the day that I decided to tell her; it was a Wednesday and my birthday. When I told her my news, I expected her to be not only pleased but proud of me.

Instead, with a tear in her eye, she gave me an envelope to open, which she had received a couple of days before and had hidden the contents from me.

I noticed that the envelope had the Redditch insignia on the front. My heart was beating hard and fast as I withdrew the letter inside. In essence, it said that they had found a place for her in an OAP's home which was miles away, at Upton on Severn, in the middle of nowhere.

However, it said it would be for a two week trial, and transport was to pick her up that weekend. I was devastated.

Apparently, she had been approached by the council during my last few weeks in the Army, and they had done a great selling job on her. The council's reason for this approach never became apparent until weeks later.

My mother cried constantly, and was racked with guilt, and her sisters never pulled any punches on how they felt about it.

That weekend, I went with her to Upton, with a suitcase full of her needs for her two week appraisal of the home. What we saw shocked us both. My mother, although elderly, had been and was very active both physically and mentally. What greeted us was row upon row of elderly and mostly incontinent inmates, sitting in silence staring ahead at nothing. She seemed to suddenly regain a spring in her step and demanded to be taken back home, which I did. I had hoped that would be the end of it, but it wasn't to be. Within days they offered her a place in a newly built complex in our town, which catered for the able bodied, and with the promise of helping out the staff and the chance of earning pocket money. This she felt she couldn't refuse. I think it was the thought of being helpful and productive which swayed her decision.

The council moved fast. Within a couple of weeks they sent me a letter of eviction, stating in no uncertain terms that I had no rights for tenancy as my name was not on the rent book, even though it had been my home all of my life.

Eugene quickly saw the advantage of pressing his thoughts on an adventure in Jersey.

I had to make up my mind. Do I stay and fight the council for a place to live, or do I put all my cares behind me and travel with my friends to the Channel Islands? No contest!

I did however think that I would out manoeuvre the council by paying six weeks rent in advance, in case I wanted to come back.

Eugene had a lot of the qualities of Paul, in so much as being someone you wouldn't want to tangle with, a good person to watch your back in the case of trouble and with the air of a silent strength. He is what you would have called a 'Man's man'.

One night, which was a Friday 13th, I told Eugene that I was superstitious and was staying in. He said that I couldn't as it was Barry's going away do at the Unicorn.

Barry was a Karate enthusiast and the local papers had made a major story out of the fact that he was about to hitch hike to Japan to further his ability in the art. So along with the Karate club of Redditch, Eugene, who worked with Barry and I, were invited to his going away party at the Unicorn.

It was a great night, and we all finished up at the chip shop which was over the road from the pub.

Not far from the chip shop there is a small wall, just right for sitting on. The twelve of us were sitting on the wall in a line, with Eugene and myself sitting on the end.

I remember Eugene saying, "Well I told you it's a silly superstition, this Friday the thirteenth rubbish. It's half eleven and it's been a great night, even though there's been no women involved."

He spoke too soon!

Now, I need to paint a picture of the protagonist of the night.

There was a Scottish family who were always in trouble with the police, mainly for fighting. Not many weeks before they had been arrested for breach of the peace. The story goes that they were in the same chippy that we had just visited, buying fish and chips and carrying a wooden case full of beer bottles, as was their custom.

As they were being served, a coach pulled up outside full of jubilant anglers who had just won a fishing competition. Half a dozen of the happy anglers came into the chip shop, singing and holding a large cup in the air above their heads. As they started to order, the Scottish contingent asked to look at the cup, which the anglers assented to.

Problem was that when the anglers wanted to get back on the coach, the yobs had filled it to the top with their booze, and wouldn't return it until they had drunk every last drop.

After a lot of arguing and pleading, it was obvious that they were reluctant to let go of their newly acquired trophy. As soon as the remaining coach passengers realised what was happening they came into the shop in force and were very angry. This was just what the yobs wanted, to instigate a fight.

Before anyone was too seriously hurt, the police arrived and arrested them. This was the norm with this family. It was known that they got away with most of their antics because the general public were frightened of repercussions.

Anyway, back to our fateful night.

As I said, all twelve of us were eating our fish and chips, in a line, on the wall. Everyone was in a good mood, when around the corner came three of the Scots, two brothers and a cousin, carrying their usual crate of beer and following close behind were their female partners.

At the end of our line, near the corner, one of the karate club members jokingly said, "How about selling us a bottle of beer?"

The two carrying the crate placed it in a shop doorway, and turned to the club member and said, "You can have one if you fight us for it."

As he said it he took off his jacket. The karate member tried to cool the situation in a light hearted way, saying he wanted no trouble, but before he could finish the sentence, the one brother downed him with his first punch, and his sibling put the boot in before he had even hit the deck. The cousin charged in, kicking him in the head. Although it had all happened so fast, not one of the karate club either moved or spoke. You could feel their fear.

Eugene and I ran past the fear frozen club members to help the victim, and as we got closer we could see some dark liquid oozing out of his ears and they were still kicking him. Both Eugene and I got in between the prone victim and the three maniacs. We tried to hold them back, and you might think that they would have turned their anger on to us, but no! They were fixated on their helpless prey.

I had a brainwave to divert their attention. I left Eugene briefly and ran over to where they had put the beer crate. I picked up a bottle and shouted, "If you don't want it then I'll have it," and pretended to drink it. I knew it would grab their attention, but the onslaught when it came was instant and ferocious. I remember Eugene and Barry carrying the unconscious kid away just as I was felled to the ground. It seemed that they used me as a human football for ages, but in reality it could have only been seconds.

I was arrested and put into the police car with two of the protagonists. The police station was only about two hundred yards away. Now, I'm no snitch, but when they started threatening me in the police car with what they would do if I didn't keep my mouth shut, it was like throwing down a gauntlet.

A week or so later, I, along with the three Scots, was up in front of the Magistrates for a breach of the peace. When they read the charge out for me to plead Innocent or Guilty, I opened my mouth to answer, but like a flash a Police Inspector, who I hadn't noticed in court before then, suddenly sprang to his feet and said all charges against me were dropped as I was giving Queen's evidence.

All through the hearing the one lady magistrate never took her eyes off me. Eugene asked afterwards if I had noticed her staring at me all the way through. I explained to him that this was the first time that I had seen her since I was five, and that when I was abandoned as a baby she had publicly announced in the local press that if none of the general public were to step forward to adopt me, then she would.

It must have been a shock to her system to find me standing in front of her.

It was only a matter of a couple of weeks later that saw us heading off to Jersey and living an unbelievable fun packed adventure, where as a group, we became legends in our own lifetime.

# Chapter 12
## The Jersey Years

There were four of us who left Redditch on that sunny Monday morning, each filled with excitement and apprehension. We each carried our hopes for the future, but Don also carried with him everything which wasn't fixed down from his rented room, which included the front door bell.

Eugene and Seamus made him ditch this as soon as we stepped off the bus. It was so embarrassing as every little bump the bus encountered made the door bell chime loud and clear, and brought us funny looks from every passenger on the short trip from Redditch to Birmingham.

We arrived in Weymouth and caught the ferry, with its dirt cheap booze and cigarettes. It was a different world to what we had expected. The nine hour journey passed very quickly. We each bought two hundred fags and passed the time away playing cards, using the cigarettes to gamble with instead of money.

When we arrived on the island our first priority was to find a place to stay, but with limited money all we could afford was a local hostel, and luckily for us the main doors were left open 24/7. When our money had gone after about two weeks, me and Don crept into the hostel late each night, put an out of order sign on the bathroom door and took it in turns to sleep in the bath, letting the other one sleep on the floor. Luckily the WC was separate, and not many residants took a bath after midnight.

Seamus and Eugene had enough money to afford a bed to sleep in during the first month or so, and regularly bought us a meal and gave us a small amount of money, which was a life saver.

One very relevant situation was myself being befriended by an Irish man, John and his wife Margret. They were hippies in the early sixties and had met on a Kibbutz in Israel, and later got married and moved to Jersey. They were die hard atheists, but I have never met a more Christian couple: they would give their last to anybody, even strangers. They allowed me to use their address to have my Army reservist pay sent to, and other correspondence, such as a reply that I had from the Redditch council.

The council had ignored my six week advanced rent payment, and informed me that I had a certain date to empty my house before it was to be demolished. The shock was that I had received the letter two days after the proposed demolition date.

The reason they had enticed my mother to give up her tenancy was to make way for the New Town development. I was gutted.

We came to a watershed as far as money was concerned. Without jobs we realised that all four of us were doomed to leave the island at the end of the next weekend.

Eugene, who spent a lot of his time in the bookies, surprised us that he had put every last penny he and Seamus possessed on Nijinsky in the Derby. I never understood betting, but apparently he had taken a really good price on the race at a previous time that week.

Nijinsky came good and it meant that our enforced leaving of the island was postponed a few days more. However, Seamus surprised us all by informing us that he would be leaving Jersey and going to Birmingham to stay with friends. He left us with his share of the horse winnings, plus as much as he could afford to help us through the next few days.

It's surprising what you will eat to survive. I remember Don getting excited when he spotted a loaf of bread underneath a parked car. It must have fallen off a bread van, the package was undamaged, and the bread felt and tasted fresh.

This was a welcome change to how we normally fed ourselves, with a needs must philosophy. Usually we would hang about outside cafe's, looking nonchalant, but in reality one of us would be scrutinising the tables inside, waiting for families to finish eating, and providing the plates had a reasonable amount of food on them we would spring into action. It was all about timing. When the diners were preparing to leave, we would be seated at the departed customers table the second that they vacated their seats. In a matter of seconds the leftovers would be gone. To keep matters looking legit, one of us would buy a large coffee, which we would secretly share.

Our days had been taken up with each morning sitting in job agencies waiting for work to come in. I remember one time that I made a complete laughing stock of myself.

I put it down to frustration and desperation. Along with a varied assortment of desperate job seekers awaiting a chance to find work, any work, we were all waiting in a long corridor. The office door at the far end of the corridor opened, and a young woman came out and shouted, "Has anyone here had any experience as a silver service waiter or waitress?"

I had been too far away to hear properly, so in my enthusiasm to land a job, I jumped up, lied, and said, "Yes, I've been a self-service waiter."

I knew I had made a faux-pas, when everybody fell about laughing. I dashed out of the building in sheer embarrassment, but in fact this turned out to be a lucky break in more ways than one.

I went to another agency and signed up straightaway, and immediately landed a job as a kitchen porter. The other major benefit was that what I had said in the previous agency soon swept the island. Being one of the handful of black people in Jersey, it was easy to recognise me as the perpetrator. This meant that I gained some standing, and people found it easier to break the ice and communicate with me and my circle of friends socially.

Young women outnumbered males by four to one, as it is in most holiday places.

So leaving the first agency turned out lucky for me, and when I met up with Don, later that day, his luck had also taken a turn for the better, as he had landed a kitchen porter's live-in job as well at the Mermaid Hotel close to the airport.

This was Don's second longest job in the first year we were there. It lasted all of two weeks, which is hard to believe. In fact, his record was seventeen jobs in the first year, which included a two week break back home and one job lasting thirty minutes for which we had a whip round for him to have a haircut, as it was a requirement for getting a landscaping job. The longest job he managed to hold on to in that period of time was just over two months.

For my part, the hotel they sent me to was rated as one of the top ranking on the island, it even had VIP dining areas and bars. Top entertainers and sports personalities were always arriving. The food was atrocious though and you wouldn't feed it to a dog.

I dropped quite a few clangers in this posh hotel when I started because I was so green. As a dishwasher my main problem was trying to get rid of some four inch shells that went out containing hors d'oeuvres. I could only crush up one at a time in the waste disposal. It was only when the disposal unit finally packed up that the head chef, who didn't have a sense of humour, kindly informed me that they were actual crockery. This all came on top of another misfortune from a couple of days before when I was instructed to tidy out the food larder.

I came across a large amount of cheeses covered in hair and all furry. The disposal unit soon got rid of them. No problem! I later explained to the head chef that no one told me that they were a delicacy. As I said, he had no sense of humour.

There were about six kitchen porters, and in the three weeks that I had worked in the kitchen, they had come and gone at very regular intervals.

They had a system of paying on the Friday lunchtime, but that included Saturday's wage.

After three weeks of working in this hell hole of a hotel, I'd had enough and was determined to leave as soon as I got my wages. What I noticed on my last Friday was that I was being followed by one of the many junior chefs. No matter where I went I had a shadow. One of the porters told me that I was seen taking a bag of clothes out late at night on the Thursday. They had assumed that I was about to do a runner that Friday. As soon as we were paid, three of the kitchen helpers absconded, and that left me and two Scouses. One of the Liverpool lads said that they had intended to leave when the others did, but their conscience made them stay, otherwise I would be have been left all on my own to cope.

They could see that I was being watched closely, so they said to be ready as they would set up a diversion, and then I could make a run for it and they would see me in the Gloucester pub later.

About half hour later, a large pot of soup fell off the burner, and everyone was startled by the noise. I quickly backed out of the kitchen, and as soon as I saw daylight I fled.

I ran all the way to the pub, and before the barman could pour my pint, the two scouse lads came in out of breath and could hardly speak through laughing.

As soon as I was spotted going out of the door, the head chef screamed out profanities, calling me all the names under the sun, and ordering the two lads to chase me and bring me back. The talk of the island that weekend was that later on that night and all day Saturday, the junior chefs were outside the hotel trying to entice passers-by to come in to help in the kitchen.

First thing Monday morning I went back to the agency, expecting them to give me a hard time and to take me off their books, but the exact opposite happened.

Like everyone else they had heard what had occurred, and reserved a relatively high paying job for me should I return. This was potato picking. The reason they supported me was due to the fact that I held the longest record as a kitchen porter that the agency had placed with this hotel.

With money in our pockets, Don, Eugene and I had many wild nights, and with the pubs having all day opening hours, we soon realised that Jersey was a rock with fifty thousand alcoholics clinging on to it.

I don't know which hotel Eugene worked and lived in, but we mainly met up with him on the night time.

It wasn't long before Eugene turned up one night with a young stranger. He looked half caste, same as me. Up until then, we had only known of one other coloured person apart from me on the island, who was a DJ. This added to the mystery of the new stranger.

Eugene dropped a bombshell when he told us that the next morning he and the young unknown stranger would be leaving the island together and going to London.

As I said he was the greatest stud I had ever known, and Jersey with its ratio of girls to blokes was his Utopia. We joked that he needed a rest and didn't want to burn himself out before middle age.

That night turned into a great going away party, but events really took a strange twist, which baffled everyone.

Earlier that day the island was full of excitement because of the expected visit of a Royal Navy warship. This was a very rare event. It was the only time that I had ever seen a Navy ship visit the island, and some people said they could never remember an occasion in the past when this had happened since the war years.

That night other friends of ours, Mickey, Helmet and Rob, joined us to wish Eugene and his new found friend a bon voyage.

When I say we were drunk, I mean *really* drunk, almost legless.

The pubs were nearly all closed, only the discos were open, but we all decided to call it a night after calling into a chippy nearby. I felt a bit sicker than the rest and said I would wait outside, which I did. The other six went inside to get the takeaways.

I was leaning against the wall by the door, trying to remain upright. Don brought out my fish and chips then went back into the shop. I had just started to eat them when I noticed a lot of shouting and arguing. I looked up, and approaching the chip shop were three people, two sailors in uniform and in between them this guy in civvies, who was obviously drunk and arguing loudly.

As they were about to pass, the guy not in uniform said to the sailors, "I never really hit him, I just went like that," and with this statement he hit me in the face. I remember my chips went flying, and my reaction was immediate, and I hit him.

He went flying backwards and fell hitting his head on the kerb. My companions came running out of the shop and got between me and the sailors. There were a lot of other people about, some were gathered around the floored person.

It was then that I looked more closely and it was apparent that he could be badly hurt as there appeared to be blood coming out of his ear. It seemed like only seconds before the police cars and an ambulance arrived. It sobered me up when I saw him being put on a stretcher and loaded into the back of the ambulance.

Eugene and the young dark stranger, plus other revellers, seemed eager to give statements to the police. One of the policemen took my details down and a brief statement. What happened next seemed unbelievable. Eugene, after speaking to the police, came over and said that the police had radioed for a cab to take me and Don to John's house, and that he and his new friend would go with the police to give a more in depth statement.

That was the last I ever saw of Eugene or his new companion. I assumed that they went to London. I never heard anymore about the incident. I did think that I should try and find out how the injured bloke was, but everyone said, "Let sleeping dogs lie." I've often wondered how he was, as there was a lot of blood coming out of his ears.

The way Eugene came into my life and then left seemed so similar to Paul's entry and departure in my life. Both men had been so close and exclusive to me and only me. They both also seemed to be able to manipulate authority at will.

Only now writing this account a thought has hit me. Did the navy vessel which left the following day, which was the same day as Eugene, have any link, or was it pure coincidence? I will never know, but the suddenness of losing a good close friend really hurt.

I should point out that there is one other person who I have not mentioned yet.

His name was Richard Garfield, and like Trevor from my Army days, remained the closest of friends a man could ever wish for. He worked at the Europa hotel, on the reception desk. He had a little quirk though. Once he had cleaned the receptionist carpet, he hated the customers standing on it. He would politely ask them to move off it, to allow the carpet to dry. I'll talk more about Richard later on.

Not long after Eugene left, the potato picking had come to an end, and I soon found work again in a couple of hotels once more as a kitchen porter.

Potato picking was very arduous work, but the money made it worthwhile.

At that time I jumped at the chance to buy a car, a very cheap old Austin 55 banger.

This allowed me and Don's close circle of friends, Micky from Worthing, Dave (Helmut) from up north, and Rob, a chef from Birmingham, to get out and about and party longer and harder than we had ever done before. Micky had taken over the reins from Eugene as the object of desire for the opposite sex. Again, it was because of his stunning looks, as they mirrored another heartthrob of the day, Paul Nicholas. With his long blonde locks, cheeky smile and southern accent, he was a natural honey pot to the ladies, but didn't capitalise on it as Eugene had done.

The last hotel that I found work in was the *West Hill,* and was by far one of the best on the island

This hotel was aimed at the lower end of the market, but stood head and shoulders above all the posh hotels, with its award winning French chef John Paul. They were easily one of the highest sought after employers, because of their standards for food and service, and they paid way and above for the best workers. For instance, there was only me and a young Liverpudlian called Kevin as kitchen porters, but we did the work of six and this was reflected in our pay. The chef gave Kevin a chance to become a chef in his own right, and he seized the opportunity with both hands. I managed to get Don the vacant position as pot washer, as again he was out of work.

Before I finished with my employment at the West Hill, I must mention a situation which occurred very frequently, which later had a profound effect on what was to happen at a much later date.

That was the regular visits by the police, one a sergeant with white hair, who was always accompanied by a constable, but rarely the same one twice. I had always assumed that the Sergeant was a close friend of the chef, John Paul, and on each visit I served them with drinks and coffee in the small staff room. At no time had I ever engaged in conversation with them. I thought it strange at the time that they never spoke to me about the incident which had occurred a few months before, with the sailors and the drunk that was whisked off in an ambulance.

Apart from my recent years and involvement with Her Majesty's forces, you would think that if I had been shadowed in the past then it would now end, but there was a situation I was now in without even being aware of it.

If nothing in my past warranted closer investigation then what was happening now certainly would.

I have said that I used John and Margret's as a postal address so that I could keep in touch with family and friends back in England. I also used their address to have my periodic Army reservist pay sent to. I never knew that the rules forbade me leaving the shores of Britain whilst being on reserve call up. In fact the Ministry of Defence wrote and told me in no uncertain terms, but allowed me to continue.

I had never been interested in politics, but that was about to change over the next few months.

Looking back at the next event must have sent shivers down our national security's spine, if you accept the fact that Eugene had been my minder or shadow. Especially as now he was no longer my constant companion. As I have said before, 'naïve' being my middle name, none of what happened during those last few years seemed apparent to me, or that my actions were of any significance.

My visits to John and Margret's were mainly to pick up my Army reservist pay and any letters. I did bump into John on odd occasions, when he was stood on street corners in St Helier handing out newspapers. I had never taken any notice at the time as to what these papers were about. This was going to change very soon.

One day John asked for a favour, and after all that he had done for me I could never have refused even if I had wanted to.

The favour he asked was to save him booking a taxi, and that could I pick up a friend of his from the Airport on a certain day. *No big deal*, I thought.

On the day in question I went to pick up this person called Devlin (Dev). He was told to look out for a coloured person, and as I was only one of two on the island it wouldn't be too difficult.

Dev was a tall, heavily built man, with a broader than normal Irish accent. He shook my hand and I bent to pick up one of his suitcases, and when I lifted it I was surprised at how heavy it was.

When we got back to John's flat, it was then that I found out what was in the suitcase. Nothing but newspapers. Not your everyday newspapers as they were titled *Irish Liberation Army.* This was an extreme arm of the IRA.

Apparently, these were the papers that John had been distributing over the months when he went downtown.

It wasn't the papers that shook me, but the conversation which followed. It seems that Dev had recently been on TV in an interview which I was told became infamous.

Dev produced photographs of the event. His interviewer was a top hard talking, controversial debater on television at that time. Not a very big person, in fact quite small with larger than life glasses. They were sitting opposite each other, just a short distance away, on black leather chairs in front of the camera, and the show was live.

During the heated debate, the very ice cool interviewer completely lost it. He sprang from his chair and smacked his studio guest in the face, and ran out of the studio.

*(I have tried to research this event on the internet, but under the Official Secrets Act there are a few things omitted in this particular interviewer's story).*

I can only tell it as I remember it being told to me. I took him back to the airport a few days later, and only picked him up once more in the time I was in Jersey, but remained filled with very mixed and confused feelings.

I was sorry to leave the hotel, but I had a chance of working for the States of Jersey Sewage Board.

I will never forget my interview with the Superintendent, a Mr McKenzie (Mac).

To land a job working for the council was the objective of any of my peers, as the wages were so good, but the fringe benefits such as sick and holiday pay were well above the norm.

I could have jeopardised my chance, when after he informed me of all my benefits and told me that I had got the job, I jumped in and said, "Thanks but I have one request, and that is that I have never worked on my birthday in my entire life and I don't want to start now." He laughed and agreed, and I was to start the following Monday.

This was to have repercussions months later, when Mac was doing one of his many rounds of inspections, and stopped to chat with Stan the foreman of the incinerators, which is where I worked. He jokingly told Stan about what I had said on my interview.

Big mistake! Stan soon got together with the other foremen and demanded that they and all other workers could have their birthdays off with pay as well. As far as I know this extra day still is in existence, as it was confirmed to me that it was fifteen years later.

The good money afforded me the chance to look for proper lodgings, but I still kept in close contact with John and Margret and their three children. Don left the West Hill now that I could help him with lodgings in the same small hotel in Gloucester Street, which was directly opposite the main hospital.

There was a pub at either end of Gloucester Street. The one situated on the corner, up by a small open park was The Adelphi. This was to become our local and the meeting place for all our nights out. At the other end of the street stood the Gloucester Vaults. This is where Jet Harris of The Shadows would perform three nights a week, for his bed and board. My and Don's lodgings were ideally situated between the two pubs.

As I have said our relatively small group lived life to the full, and we were well known in and around the island. No way should we have been called hooligans or yobs of any kind, but I did spend all three of my birthday nights locked up in a cell. Each time it was farcical and the police found it amusing as well.

Before I tell you my birthday events, you would need to know how the legal system worked.

# Chapter 13
## The Law

As far as I recall the average bobby's on the beat were seconded from the different forces in Britain, which meant at first glance their uniforms looked the same, but their helmets and badges depicted which constabulary they were from.

Uniformed police had the power of arrest, but it was the plain clothed police who were the true force. These were Centeniers and there was one from each of the 12 parishes of Jersey. They had the powers of arrest, but only they could charge you. They also had Vingteniers in plain clothes who dealt with vehicle misdemeanours.

If you were arrested by the police, then you would be taken in front of the Centenier on duty that night. This was in fact the prequel to being put in front of a Court hearing with a sitting Magistrate.

They mainly imposed fines or remanded people in jail to set or await a court date. The Centenier's were on a rota system, and being young, healthy, fun loving teens, it was easy to be brought in front of one of them from time to time!

We had thought ourselves very fortunate many times not having been brought in front of the Hanging Centenier, (as he was generally known amongst my peers). He was the legal representative for the parish of St Saviour.

He had the reputation of expelling offenders from the island for the most trivial reasons, and you were never given a second chance. He looked on it as being his duty and mission in life to rid Jersey of any riff raff. Any offence would do, no matter how small.

With the hindsight of maturity, I realised that some of the events were very stupid, and I was not proud of my actions. In fact I was very lucky not to have been locked up for a very long time, or even worse to have maimed or killed someone.

The following incidents are not in any particular order, but give an insight as to how life was.

During my time at the Westhill Hotel, Don suggested we buy a car between us, as the hotel was inland and we needed transport to get around.

All was well at first, but after a couple of months the brakes on the car failed. It would have taken months of saving to get them fixed, in fact, more than the car initially cost.

It fell to me to drive as Don didn't hold a licence.

Not only was our hotel inland, but up a long winding country road.

After a night on the town getting back was no problem, as with a couple of Portuguese and Italian waiters in the car, the weight helped to slow it down when we parked up.

Getting into St Helier was a different proposition. There was only one road that I could use with a car that had no brakes. Fortunately one of the roads leading on to the main road, which ran parallel with the esplanade, had a large hotel at the bottom of the hill. The side of the hotel had no footpath, just a long blank wall. I had perfected sliding and scraping the passenger side of the car along the side of the hotel until I was slow enough to use the handbrake. This went on for weeks.

During that time, I had many a close shave; yes, 'stupid is as stupid does'.

There were two major incidents I had whilst driving, which both seem hard to believe and show just how fortunate I was.

One of our favourite places to have a good time was the Normandie Hotel, which had a great disco every Friday night, and we looked on as our local. This was where we practised 'minesweeping'. More on that later.

This one particular night there was just me and Don tripping the light fantastic, and at the end of the night, Don felt that he had pulled, and it was hard to drag him away. It was obvious that unless he could arrange a date with the girl in question, he wasn't leaving the dance. So I agreed to wait on the car park until he was ready to go.

A group of acquaintances that we knew saw me sitting behind the wheel of the car. They soon realised that I was absolutely pissed. One of them warned me that the Police were out in force, and setting up road blocks.

Not long after the warning, a beam of light was shone on my face, blinding me. Then a voice out of the darkness asked, "Is this your car?"

"Yes," I mumbled.

"What's the registration number?"

I tried several times to get it right, but gave up. The other officer chimed up, "You've been drinking, I hope you are not thinking of driving tonight."

Quick as a flash I replied, "I'm too pissed to walk, let alone drive. I'm waiting for my mate to come out. He doesn't drink and he will be driving." With a final warning, they let it go at that.

Don came out and I quickly brought him up to speed as to what had happened. Don couldn't drive, so it was up to me to get us back. I decided to use the small back streets to avoid any road blocks. Luck was against me, and in a short while I turned into a narrow back road in the town straight into a road block. I never knew that the island had so many police. There were a couple of cars held up in front of us. My heart was thumping hard inside my chest and I even sobered up a little.

When our turn came, I was instructed to roll my window down, as was Don by the officer on his side of the car. Unfortunately, the one on my side was the same one I had just had a conversation with on the car park. He reminded me of it, but I denied that was me he had spoken to. Even when I said it, I realised how stupid it sounded.

The same policeman took both of us to the group of other officers whilst he inspected our car. Of course he had noticed the damage on my side, and called out to the others, *If he ever hit anyone with this car, it would tear them to pieces*, I thought, *he will freak out if he sees the passenger side.*

He walked around the car taking notice of the odd lights which were out, and the bald tyres. It was when he got down on his knees to look under the car that the mood with the officers changed. In fact the one who was stood by my side nudged me, nodded his head towards his colleague on his knees and muttered, "Pratt."

After the inspection was finished one of the policemen said, "Park your car over there, and don't move it until you get this list of faults fixed."

I said, "Yes sir I'll get a garage to pick it up first thing in the morning."

That next morning, I was up with the lark, and went down to retrieve my car. Never heard anymore about it.

The next time I had a similar incident, it seemed to give some logical reason as to why I got off so lightly that night. The next major event relating to the car was a couple of weeks later.

Every Sunday afternoon, all of our crowd would take three or more cars down to a music bar on the beach in St Brelades Bay. One of our drinking buddies was Terry Harris, who was more famously known in his stardom days as Jet Harris of the Shadows fame. I genuinely liked his company, but I felt that my peers, more or less, tolerated him because he would have been what is commonly known as a *Babe Magnet*. It was so easy picking up girls with him around, just like shooting fish in a barrel.

By this time I had become quite adept at driving without brakes. As per normal we would all travel back in the early evening.

This Sunday in question, after a heavy drinking session, me, Don and a couple of others had travelled back to town at about 10 pm. Unfortunately, it was at this time of night that the police sealed off certain roads with portable fencing for some traffic reason or other.

I planned on parking the car around the corner of Gloucester Street, up by the Adelphi pub.

As I turned the corner I came across two policemen who had just finished off sealing the road a street away. It wasn't the fact that I had mounted the pavement turning out of Gloucester Street that turned their attention towards me, it was because I had forgotten to put my lights on. The two policemen flagged me down and immediately suspected that I had been drinking. They evicted my passengers and the young policeman told me to get in the passenger seat as he thought me incapable of driving. He said he wanted me tested for alcohol.

116

As he started to drive off, I held my breath and thought, *Shall I warn him about the lack of brakes?* As I was perusing the situation, he shot across the street in front of an on coming car screaming, "There's no brakes."

I quickly said, "I thought something had gone wrong. That's why I mounted the kerb."

I gave him his due; he nursed the car a couple of hundred yards back to the main police station.

We went through the main swing doors together, and in front of us, behind the long reception desk, stood a sergeant who I recognised from my Westhill days.

Everything happened so quickly. The sergeant said to my police escort, "What's up with him?"

"I want him to see the doctor," replied my arresting officer.

"He looks all right to me," the desk sergeant said.

The young policeman looked at me and said, "Piss off then, but your car stays here." I've never moved so fast.

That was the last time that I saw my car. I phoned up the next morning from my digs, and told them I wouldn't have enough money to get it repaired, so could they dispose of it. That's the last I ever heard about the incident.

# Chapter 14
## Being Youthful or Just Plain Stupid

My first encounter with the Hanging Centenier was a serious matter as far as the law in Jersey was concerned. They would never tolerate yobbish drunken behaviour. It was paramount to keep the island a safe place for holidaymakers, so if you were ever arrested for a drunken, or especially violent act, then you knew that you would be dealt with harshly.

As I have said we had thought ourselves very fortunate many times not having been brought in front of him. He was the legal representative for the parish of St Saviour.

He had the reputation of expelling offenders from the island for the most trivial reasons, and you were never given a second chance. He looked on it as being his duty and mission in life, to rid Jersey of any riff raff. Any offence would do, no matter how small.

The Normandie Hotel was our favourite for nights out, as there always seemed to be more eligible women there on dance nights. We got on well with the staff, especially the bouncers, which was a great aid if ever we got caught 'minesweeping'.

Luckily though, their services were never needed, and they were ignorant as to what we got up to.

However they did come to my aid over another matter, when I was arrested and locked up on my birthday celebration night.

What had happened was that our tight-knit group had gone out particularly early this one Friday night to have a few, or more than a few, drinks for my birthday. Later that night, as usual, we intended to finish up at the Normandie. As we approached the car park, we noticed a bit of a disturbance at the hotel entrance. A fairly large group of Scots, who seemed the worse for wear, were screaming and shouting at the doorman because they were being refused entry.

They saw us approaching and cleared a way through the drunken howling mob to let us in. Out of the blue the bouncers suddenly stopped Don and said that there was a new rule that, on the main nights, ties had to be worn. The bouncers knew that we would leave if Don was excluded, but before we started to object to this new rule, one of the doormen took me to one side and explained the situation. The noisy bunch of Scots outside were really being excluded because they were paralytic through drink. The staff used the excuse to bar them, as none of them had ties on.

He then suggested that I go up to the first landing, and climb out of the window onto the large flat roof which was over the main entrance. There I could throw my tie down to Don at the side of the building. The bouncer said that I would need his help to climb out of the window as the bottom was six feet off the floor. Coming back through the window was at waist level, so I wouldn't have a problem.

Of course he hadn't taken into account how much I'd had to drink, so I wasn't as agile as normal. The hardest part was getting Don's attention without alerting the mob as to what our plan was. Eventually the plan worked and Don put my tie on and was allowed in.

What happened next was entirely my fault, I should have gone straight back in through the window, after the mission was completed.

It was a humid night and I lit a fag, soaked up the nights cool air, and even had a little solo dance to the music of The O' Jays 'Love Train' drifting up from the bowels of the hotel. By the time I was ready to come back into the hotel, the commotion at the front entrance had subsided, but with the bouncer now not at the window base I was concerned. I was a bit apprehensive of the six foot drop on to the landing floor, but I needn't have worried as waiting for me were two of Jersey's finest. The first said, "Who do you think you are, the Pink Panther?"

The other one said, "You been out for a walk? They have doors downstairs for that sort of thing." I couldn't find my helpful bouncer or remember his name, so they whisked me off in the panda car. I spent my first birthday on the island in a cell. It wasn't to be my last!

At least I wasn't taken in front of the Hanging Centenier.

The next morning the hotel manager, after finding out what had happened, visited the police station and asked the question, "Why would he break in, when he had already paid his entrance." So with that I was set free, and asked for an apology. They fell about laughing, and I left.

The first time that I had the misfortune to be brought in front of the Hanging Centenier was quite a serious offence by Jersey's standards, as it involved drunkenness and violence, and I was convinced that Don and I would be deported. At least it gave the court officials a good laugh.

Again it was a birthday night and by our standards very uneventful, that is until we rounded the night off with a late bite to eat and a cup of coffee.

Me, Mickey, Helmut and Don called into this popular restaurant. It was opposite the town hall. Its layout was unusual as it was very long but very narrow, with single tables either side of the narrow aisle. Mick and Helmut were sitting opposite me and Don.

We ordered four coffees and each chose a meal from the menu.

The restaurant was extra busy as we drank our coffee's and the time ticked on to a point where we had forgotten about the meals we had ordered.

We were having such a laugh. I should mention that although we always dressed fairly smart, Mick's dress was always impeccable and was the catalyst for what followed.

We were really enjoying our banter as only drunks could do, when suddenly Don picked up the squeegee tomato sauce dispenser, which was red coloured and shaped like a giant tomato. For no reason at all Don pointed it at Mick, who looked horrified. This was to be expected as he was wearing his brand new suede jacket which he had bought earlier that day, and cost him most of his wages. He threatened Don, and like us believed that Don wouldn't be that stupid.

Wrong. The stream of thick sauce he directed at his blonde wavy locks. The effect of this was electric, and for a couple of seconds we just sat there in silence awaiting Mick's reaction. You could see he was angry and ready to explode.

He said in cold anger, staring straight at Don, "I suppose you think that's funny," but as he said it, the pool of sauce had moved onto his forehead and then accelerated down his face and was dripping off his nose. It was only the fact that Mick's straight angry face, covered in ketchup, made the situation surreal and extremely funny, which broke the ice.

Mick grabbed the brown sauce and drenched Don, while Helmut and I fought over the ketchup dispenser and not only soaked ourselves, but the other two. Looking back we must have caught innocent diners in our affray.

We weren't thinking straight, and although being the worse for wear because of drink, we were all feeling embarrassed. We decided to leave and call it a night. We walked the long length of the narrow restaurant to pay for our coffees at the till situated by the door. As Mick was paying I heard a shouting in a foreign language. I looked up the long length of the restaurant and saw an agitated young Spanish waiter running towards us. Before we knew it, he took a big kick at Don on his kneecap, which felled him in agony. He was still screaming and shouting, and I said angrily, "If you want to try kicking me, come outside."

He grabbed my collar and dragged me out of the door. I hit him. He held his nose and ran back inside. We shrugged off the incident and proceeded to walk home. We had walked a couple of streets when two police cars screeched to a halt. We found ourselves surrounded by uniformed officers. I always remember the first officer to speak saying, "We had an APB to look out for four youths covered in sauce, so you weren't hard to find."

It was when we found out that the Hanging Centenier was on duty we knew our days on the island were soon coming to an end.

It was only whilst being questioned that we found out what had caused the waiter to become agitated. We had forgotten about the meal we had ordered. Given the chance we would have paid whether we had eaten it or not.

The Centenier found us guilty and fined us on the spot. He commented on our previous record and said it was our last chance (which was more than a surprise). We had to agree to pay the fine or go to Jail over the weekend. It was a hefty fine, so Don elected to go to jail and face court on the Monday morning.

The court case was a farce, as when I stated that the waiter had come out of the kitchen at the back of the restaurant to assault us, the Magistrate seemed to be leaning to our side of the case. Every time they asked him where he had come from before the assault, all he would repeat was, "Barcelona" or "Spain". In the end, amidst all the laughter Don was given a bigger fine than me, and if he couldn't pay he would be deported back to England.

Luckily I had managed to get a job for Don at the Sewage Board a couple of weeks earlier, so money wasn't going to be a problem.

Believe it or not, we were back in front of the same Centenier within a matter of weeks.

This time it was Don's birthday, and after a few warm up drinks we had arranged to meet up with another group of friends to celebrate. We were to meet them in a Beer Keller, which I believe was in the basement of the *Royal Yacht Hotel.*

What I was unaware of was a bet that Mick and Don had struck with each other earlier on and that was that Don couldn't smuggle out one of the many small plaques on the walls advertising various lagers.

I remember it being a great night with the beer flowing freely, and a good night was had by all, but Sandy Cooper was always there and was like a steadying force on our antics.

At closing time we were all gathered outside the entrance of the Beer Keller, but in separate small groups, along with a batch of other groups of revellers.

At this point I still had no idea where Don was, but I happened to look up, and I saw him getting into a car. I broke away from the crowd, muttering, "The bastards got himself a taxi without telling me, see you lot tomorrow," and off I sped down the road. I just reached the car as it had started to pull away. I yanked the door open and jumped into the back seat beside Don. I immediately started cursing him out for getting a taxi without telling me.

At that split moment I realised that the two occupants in the front both had uniforms on. "Oops," I said trying to leave.

"If you're his friend you can stay," said one of the coppers.

What had happened was that earlier on Don had pulled a plaque out from under his jumper and was waving it about in the air and taunting Mickey, by saying, "Right, you owe me a pound for the bet, but if you want it, it will be an extra pound."

Apparently, everyone was too drunk and not aware of the two policemen standing nearby. They arrested Don after taking the plaque off him and had radioed for transport.

Just our luck, when we reached the Town Hall we found out that the Hanging Centenier was on duty that night. We both realised that this was probably going to be our last night in Jersey, especially after the dressing down we had been given on the previous occasion before him. Neither of us was prepared for what was about to happen.

He interviewed us together, and we listened to what the arresting officer had to say. When he spoke it was in a grave voice and said, "I think you two have too much money to spend, so therefore I fine you two pounds each."

I quickly retorted, "I only got in the police car because I thought it was a taxi."

He replied, "All right, a pound for you." No lecture or warning,that was it.

We had never felt more relieved.

# Chapter 15
## Miss Channel Islands

This tit bit was one of the funniest situations that I have ever witnessed. However, you do have to put yourself in an imaginative frame of mind. I just hope I can do it justice, as the old saying goes, you had to have been there.

Don was still working his way through his many short term jobs, but at this one time he was in between jobs. Our landlady came into the lounge, all excited holding the local newspaper in her hand. It was the early edition.

She had found an advertisement marked urgent '*Waiters Wanted*'. Seeing Don had tried every other possible avenue for work, she suggested he gave it a try as the advert looked and sounded desperate.

It was late afternoon when Don phoned the number out of the paper, and he looked excited when he put the phone down. I had never seen him excited about getting a job before.

He pushed his long greasy unkempt hair out of his eyes, and we could see his eyes were sparkly and alive. He took a deep breath and said, "They are desperate, it involves being a bar waiter at tonight's *Miss Channel Island's* beauty competition." It was being filmed live on Channel TV.

His excitement subsided a little when he told us that he had to promise to arrive by 7 o'clock, dressed in black trousers, black shoes, a white shirt and a dark bow tie.

All of us in the little hotel's lounge that Saturday morning realised the Herculean challenge before us. Who could we borrow a white shirt off? It would probably be easier to find a virgin on the island. Still we made phone calls, and a few went out to see if they could find someone who could help, not only for a shirt but for a bow tie.

To be kind to Don he wasn't one of the world's smartest dressers; it just wasn't in his nature.

Time started to run out fast. One of our searchers managed to locate a bow tie. Unfortunately, it wasn't black, but a dark purple and its size was a problem. In fact it was the largest one that any of us had seen.

No one could come up with what we thought would be the easiest item: trousers.

Someone said to me that I used to wear black trousers to work. This was true, but working on the incinerators they were badly scorched, almost see through in places and badly needed pressing. The landlady grabbed the trousers off me and disappeared into the kitchen to sponge and press them. There was so much positive energy being emitted all around that I didn't want to be a party pooper and mention that Don was a good four inches taller than me.

Now came the crucial problem: a white shirt, and when I look back on what developed it shows just how desperate we had become.

Again someone said to me that I wear a whitish shirt at work, but this time I said, "You gotta be kidding me, have you seen it?"

It had been white years earlier, and I should have binned it a long time ago, but now it was more off cream, and worst of all the collar had become so stained with ash and sweat no one in their right mind would want to wear it.

I had no idea who came up with the scatty suggestion of taking the top layer of material off the collar, and said that the material underneath should be whiter than the actual stained collar. Wrong!

Time had almost run out for us to get Don to the prestigious event.

All we needed now was someone else to come up with an even scattier brainwave, but there just has to be one.

We couldn't leave the collar as it was, so we were forced to try the stupidest idea since the Captain of the Hindenburg said let's go out for a smoke.

Yes, let's use toothpaste to cover up the stains, so we did. Don was instructed to try and keep his head still whilst working, and definitely not to turn his head if he could help.

Don had begged me to go in with him when we got there for moral support. As we were all broke he said if I could get in then he would see that he would keep a free beer flowing for me.

As we got into the car in Gloucester Street, I was hoping that the hysterical laughter which I could hear flowing from our digs wasn't going to unsettle him. I got him in the car as soon as possible, then excused myself to go back into the hotel to pop to the toilet. In reality I needed to let my emotions out. I was actually crying when I got back in the car, but I don't think Don noticed; well he couldn't turn his head could he.

I didn't realise then that I was about an hour and a half from my funniest moment on the island.

We got to the venue, West Park Pavilion, just a short drive away, and when we got there Don asked to be introduced to his intended contact for the job as waiter. I for my part made sure that I entered a reasonable distance behind Don. He was whisked off to an ante room to be given instructions and to be issued with his little white jacket. He later said they nearly gave him his marching orders when he had difficulty inserting the rings which hold the buttons on, so he used matchsticks instead.

I carried on walking into the hall, just to have a look as I had never been in this building before and at this time there were no paying patrons

A man dressed in black tie apparel shook my hand and guided me up the stairs, where I was greeted by two men and a woman who were all stood drinking. The man asked what I normally drank, I replied a Mary Anne bitter. The barman heard this and pulled a pint for me and walked away without asking for money.

My three new found friends suggested that we grab a table near the front of the circle. After a lot of small talk I realised that they thought I was one of them, an invited reporter from England. As the drinks were freely flowing, I kept stum, I never felt guilty, and I hadn't lied.

Soon the auditorium began to fill up with a buzz and people in their fineries hoping to be seen on telly at this prestigious event. The circle were I was sitting was now full, and I noticed the usher who had brought me up counting heads.

Next he was over at our table asking what newspaper was I representing and could he see my Press Pass. I couldn't blag it, and told him it was just a mistake. He cordially escorted me downstairs and found me a table to sit at.

I noticed three TV cameras in the hall.

Now we come to one of the funniest moments that I can remember. No sooner had I been settled that without warning all the lights were dimmed and a voice came out of the darkness welcoming patrons to the show.

All of a sudden this ultra-bright searchlight lit up the Master of Ceremonies on the stage. He gave his normal speech and at the end of it he announced that there were plenty of bar waiters situated all around the room. As if preordained his light went out and this other ultra-bright light flashed on a well dressed waiter who stood like a statue with his silver tray held shoulder high. "Here," came the voice in the darkness, "and here." The light quickly lit up the next waiter, then again and again and when the light hit Don's post the whole auditorium erupted in laughter. His trousers four inches above his old unclean shoes, his large purple bow tie streaked with dripping toothpaste and his jacket buttoned up wrongly, and worst of all was his unruly hair covering most of his face. It wouldn't have been so bad if the operator on the torchlight instead of carrying on around to the other posts went straight back to Don who had apparently took the opportunity in the brief darkness to finish buttoning his jacket up.

I am sure the searchlight operator, along with the audience thought it was a comedy spot. This time the laughter was thunderous. I really felt sorry for him.

I didn't wait around for any free drinks off Don, and drove back to the hotel to tell the others the tale. We all thought, oh well, he will at least he will have earned a night's wages, but a matter of minutes later Don came in looking angry and hurt.

He had been sacked for losing the buttons of his jacket.

Laughing, we nearly died!

# Chapter 16
## The States of Jersey

To land a job working for the council was the objective of any of my peers as the wages were good, but the fringe benefits such as sick and holiday pay were well above the norm.

The sewage board was a great place to work, and the alternating eight hour shifts suited me down to the ground. What I loved most of all were the many types of people that I would come into contact with.

There was George, who was a coloured labourer and who always had his best friend with him, a hard bristle broom. He was always talking to it as if it was a human being. Sometimes he could be heard arguing with his broom, especially if it wasn't performing up to his standard. So George made up a surprising and unexpected threesome of black residents on the island. The reason we had never seen him about at night was because he played in a band, performing in gigs at some of the top hotels. I remember him telling us once that his showbiz career came crashing down when he couldn't help himself imitating *Johnny Mathis* and the way he talked whilst he was in the backing group when the singer toured Britain.

Then there was Mick Donavon, a proud Irishman from Dublin, generous of character, whose face was heavily scarred. He was short and very stocky and drank Guinness like it was going out of fashion. As I said he drank a lot, which left his face a constant cherry red except for the large rectangle on his forehead. This was because the steel plate in his skull remained white as the skin graft never changed colour. He was proud of his wounds, which came about when he was a young teenager riding a motorbike as a delivery/mailman for the IRA, and was ambushed by the *Black & Tans* during the Irish civil war.

I keep using the word proud, but no other word fits. The following event shows what I mean.

Every night when our shift finished at ten, we had to rush to his local so that he could down his minimum four pints of Guinness before the pub closed at eleven.

This one night as Mick was downing his second pint, the barman asked him if he had read in that day's paper of the new record for drinking so many Guinness's in a certain time. Mick said, "No." That wasn't a problem, but when the barman told him it was some Welsh bloke, Mick looked like he was going to burst into tears, turned and walked out of the pub. He was inconsolable, and never turned up to work for the rest of the week.

Another character on my six man shift was Roger, of Polish extraction, who actually did breakdown in the same pub a few weeks later. What made this episode alarming was that Roger was a great workmate, quiet and unemotional.

This certain night we had all rushed to our local pub to down as many pints as usual before closing time. We were all standing at the bar so that we didn't waste drinking time having to move forwards and backwards to order our beer. Roger was unusually mute and didn't engage in the banter going on between the rest of us. He just stood there with his eyes fixed on the television above the bar, which was showing black and white footage of naval warfare during the Second World War. None of us took any notice of the programme, it was just white noise to us.

Getting near to closing time, someone said, "Look at Roger, he's crying." We were shaken to see tears streaming, his face transfixed on the telly. We knew something wasn't right. We gently took him to a table in a corner of the pub, and sat him down.

We slowly coaxed it out of him. The programme on the TV was a documentary about the sinking of the German battleship, 'The Bismark'. This ship was one of Germany's great successes in the war, causing havoc and destruction amongst Allied shipping.

Roger sat there sobbing and explained that he was on a submarine for a great many months. Their one objective was to sink the Bismark. The crew, like him, were so geared up and lived for the day that they were to be engaged in combat with this prolific ship.

The Bismark was undergoing repairs in one of the many Norwegian fjords whilst being protected by heavy support ships and land artillery. Roger's shipmates, knowing that they may be giving up their lives at any minute, had laid in wait at the entrance to the fjord where the Bismark had entered waiting for intelligence reports of it setting sale back to the Atlantic.

When the news did arrive, after what seemed a lifetime, it crushed the submariners.

The Bismark left the fjords in an unexpected outlet and was sunk by the Royal Navy. The TV programme had a profound effect on Roger.

There was one other workmate who I had the uppermost respect for, his name was Dave. He knew that I wanted to go back home for a summer break, and that I couldn't afford the travel fare. His solution was to sell me his Lambretta scooter for the grand sum of £10, and on top of that he loaned me the ferry fare, for me to repay him when I returned from England.

My trip didn't go without incident. I loved my scooter, even though I always felt that I was a Rocker and not a Mod.

I rode from Weymouth, northwards to Birmingham, on a glorious sunny day. When I had passed Oxford on a quiet peaceful dual carriageway near Abingdon, I heard a distant purr of motorbike engines, which gradually became louder and louder until it became a deafening roar.

I looked over my shoulder, and what I saw was about twenty to thirty heavy duty customised bikes. A shiver went right through me, as by their dress code it was obvious that they were *Hell's Angels.* I was shaking so much it was difficult to keep control of my trusted steed. They followed me for miles blocking off the two lane highway in the process. I just didn't know what was going to happen next.

One of the leading bikers, who I assumed was the main man, drew alongside me in the adjacent lane. He kept looking over at me, and when he did, all I could think to do in response to the situation was to smile at him.

No words passed between us, but I just knew that he accepted me as one of them, and after a couple of minutes he raised his hand and accelerated away at speed. The large group responded and in a matter of seconds they were just specks on the horizon. I did notice that their jackets were emblazoned '*Abingdon Chapter*'. What was strange was that not one of them glanced in my direction as they passed.

There were so many characters that I could recall, but one last incident worth a mention was concerning our mate Mick from Worthing. As I said, working for the States had many benefits, one of them being the generous sickness leave on full pay, which many took full advantage of. Mick was over the moon when he put in a transfer to be reemployed on the port as a grease monkey, maintaining amongst other things the dockside cranes.

All was going well until he was informed that his parents were due to come over at short notice. He was in a panic: he had no holiday left and had used up all of his sick days entitlement. What could he do?

Mick came up with a cunning plan to gain a few days off.

He needed to execute this plan when the tide in the harbour was at its fullest. This left a drop of eight to ten feet from the quay edge to the water.

The cranes were on the opposite side of the dock to that of the foreman's hut. The plan was, with the help of a lookout man, he would climb up one of the cranes with his grease gun, and when the lookout informed him that the foreman was looking out of the window, he would fake an accident by throwing himself off and into the water, screaming as loudly as possible.

The perfect time had arrived, and the lookout shouted, "Mick he's looking!" Right on cue he threw himself off backwards, screaming loudly as he did so, still holding on to his grease gun. I wasn't there but I was told it was impressive and worthy of an Oscar.

The total height he fell must have been thirty feet at least.

He eventually surfaced and quickly looked across at the foreman's office, and felt devastated when he saw that his boss had his back to the window. Dripping wet, a few of his workmates helped him back onto dry land.

You had to applaud his tenacity, he wasn't going to give up. He grabbed another grease gun and started up again. This time he reasoned he would go even higher, with more of a chance to be seen.

Once again the scene was to be replayed. The shout went up again, his scream was louder and the splash he made, I was told, was magnificent.

This time it seemed everything went according to plan, well nearly. Yes, the foreman was looking out of the window. He had also been looking the time before.

So just as Mick broke the water surface, the ambulance arrived.

The upshot was that Mick had plenty of free time to entertain his family as he was sacked on the spot!

Before I finish reminiscing about the sewage works, I feel that I must tell the tale relating to the Sewage Board's annual trip. Every year they would go to 'Lessay Fair,' which is a small coastal town, a short distance away in France.

I had managed to get a job at the works for Don in the water treatment department. He also decided to buy a second-hand scooter, but his was a Vespa.

The morning of our outing we were all to meet up in the early hours at Gorey harbour

Both Don and I went down together on our respective scooters and left them chained up on the dockside, and awaited the arrival of the rest of our workmates. This was a men only mission. We had heard of many wild tales emanating from past Lessay trips.

When all that were coming had arrived, we boarded the small ferry. Some of the old hats had brought a good supply of liquor with them to make the trip more comfortable.

Although the fair had a small amount of traditional rides, such as dodgem cars and the like, the majority of stalls were coconut shies, wheels of fortune, apple bobbing and similar attractions. Seems fairly droll doesn't it? But here is the twist.

Conventional fairs offer cuddly toys, fish in bowls etc., but Lessay was basically an agricultural/horticultural event for local farmers getting together for a good time. Most of the prizes that could be won were either alcohol or meat related. There were even drinking competitions in which you could win even more booze. Crazy! I still can't work it out.

There were so many bars, barbeques and pig roasts going on, and plenty of women dancing, including single and team combatants. It reminded one of what life was like in medieval times.

By noon we were all well past walking the white line limit, and we knew this as there was even a competition for it.

We were truly wasted, with all the cheap bottles of plonk that we had won. We had all slowed down and were slumped on the grass, taking shade where possible from the hot summer sun.

After a while someone said, "Hey Don what you got in that bag?" Don very reluctantly, but proudly, pulled out a joint of ham that he had won.

In a matter of minutes we were transformed from being a lethargic drunken group into a rabble of rebel rousers playing football in the dusty part of the ground. The game had brought us alive, and when we'd had enough, the joint of ham looked in a sorry state and it had begun to stink. So it was tossed into a bin, and we carried on around the fair, drinking more sensibly and pacing ourselves.

The time came for us to board the coach which was to take us back to the ferry. During the short journey, the windows were opened because of the rancid smell on board the bus. You didn't have to be Sherlock Holmes to realise that the coat Don had carried around with him was hiding the joint of ham that he had retrieved from the bin

If the windows could have been opened wide enough, it would have been thrown out, but Don was warned that if it found its way on board the little ferry it would find its way overboard, and Don with it!.

When we reached the ferry Don was first off the bus. He ran to the edge of the dock and threw the wrapped package into the waters at the front of the boat.

Most of us suffered sea sickness on the way back, and one of the two toilets soon became unusable as the floor was swamped with flushed water due to it being blocked.

When we disembarked, most of our fellow revellers had family and friends waiting on the dock to take them home, but after discharging most of my bodily fluids overboard during the trip I felt well enough to ride my scooter back. Also, I didn't think it safe to leave it overnight. Don asked for a lift back as he didn't think he was capable of handling his scooter. We decided to pick it up the next morning.

Don asked me to hang on so that he could nip back on board to urgently go to the toilet. I was gob smacked when he returned with the joint of ham, which we all thought he had ditched over the dock wall. Apparently, he had retrieved the ham from a bin at the fair and placed it in a smaller rubbish filled bag which he had concealed under the coat which he was carrying. When he left the coach, taking advantage of the failing light, he ran to where the ferry was docked, and as he passed the rear of the boat he tossed the ham on to the deck. He then continued to the front end of the ferry where he tossed the now half empty bag into the water. He then rescued the offending joint as soon as he boarded.

I asked where he had hidden it, and he said, "In the toilet." I had to assume it was in the cistern, but he wouldn't say one way or another.

It stunk and I refused point blank to put it in my pannier, so he put it in his own storage unit on the Vespa, and we would retrieve it when I dropped him back the next day.

It was close to noon the following morning when we drove to the dock, and a very hot sunny day.

I swear what happened next is true.

As we were approaching the Vespa, we both noticed that when people got near the parked bike, they would cross the road. We assumed that the cause must be the overwhelming smell, but when we got there we were wrong. It was a swarm of flies circling around the machine. I kept my distance and told Don to dispose of the joint on his way back, which he said he would. I thought that would be the end of it.

About a week later I was stunned when our landlady thanked Don for the joint of ham he gave to her a week before, and said how much her guests enjoyed it.

She did say that she had saved us some to make our sandwiches for work. You can guess where they ended up!

# Chapter 17
## The Third Man

The reason for my story is to put the facts down in my belief that over a period of four years or more, certain people came into and out of my life, each lasting approximately a year. Four in all.

It took literally decades of me telling and retelling my tidbits of stories, that many people suggested that maybe, just maybe there was a connection between them. On reflection the more that I thought about it, the more it seemed possible and even likely.

The third person who came into our group, as I have already mentioned, was Sandy Cooper, which is a name I will use to tell my story.

His involvement in my life at least left me with a way of checking with any certainty any facts to either kill or confirm my belief that I may have been shadowed by the security services. It was my wife's idea who suggested that it would prove one way or another if there was any validity in my suspicions.

Again he had the same airs and graces about him that Paul and Eugene had about them. Loyal only to me, friendly, but not at all interested in any of my friends or peers.

Quiet with an inner strength, someone you wouldn't want to cross. He smoked the occasional joint, but unlike the rest of us was not a heavy drinker, and always in control of his emotions. In looks I would compare him with a young Lee Marvin.

Men's style in the '70s was very flamboyant and colourful with patterned tailored shirts, matching ties and tight fitting flared trousers

He dressed very differently from anyone else in our age group. He always wore jeans with a sporting jacket and had a small well trimmed moustache and fair shoulder length hair. He was our anchor and steadying force

Sandy was nearly always with us on our escapades. He never stayed out late and nearly always went home early. Most of our group rented rooms, but in mine and Don's case we rented a room in a small hotel. Our landlady would make us the odd sandwiches for work from the food left over from her paying guests. Sandy, on the other hand, told us he lived with an elderly lady out in the countryside (or so he had us believe). I did pick him up once from this isolated cottage, but never glimpsed a look at his landlady. His reason for always going back early was because she went to bed early, and locked the doors at a set time.

Sandy instigated a situation which still remains the most embarrassing moment in my life. It wasn't his fault by any means, it was that he had talked me into competing in one of our many drinking competitions.

It would not have been half as traumatic if I had been drinking.

Every now and then we would have a competition as to who could drink a pint of beer the fastest. This nearly always took place at the end or close to the end of a night out.

In our group it had quite a significance and the winner stayed the champ until he was defeated. Being the champ not only gave one a kudos of high esteem, it also meant that should we, as a group, be in dispute as to where to go on a given night, then the champ cast the final vote, which was binding. It saved our merry band from fracturing when decisions were difficult.

As it happens I had held the honour for a week or two, even though Mick had challenged me for the crown on a couple of occasions. I had dodged the challenge for various reasons, and Mick and the rest of the group were becoming restless for me not taking up the challenge.

It came to a head on a late Saturday morning when we were playing cards in the *Southampton Hotel* lounge, which was on the esplanade just down from the ferry port. There were two justifiable reasons for me refusing the challenge. The one reason was that I am not good at knocking back beers unless I have had a decent drink first, and I couldn't because I had to be at work at 2 o'clock.

The main reason was the fact that I had such a bad case of gastroenteritis and I was taking pain relief for my stomach.

The argument was at the point of getting heated when Sandy suggested that I should take up the challenge with the proviso that because of these two valid reasons, should I lose the crown then I had the option of a re-challenge within 48 hours.

I felt backed into a corner I couldn't get out of.

So the scene was set. There were about eight of us sitting round the table in this posh bar. Sandy went to the bar to get the drinks in and Don had been designated as the time keeper. Don had asked Sandy to bring him back a toasted cheese sandwich with the drinks. We were all ready to start, but Don suggested we wait until he had got his sandwich before beginning.

My stomach was hurting so much that my belt was cutting into me and I knew I wasn't fit for purpose, so I accompanied Sandy to the bar to see if they had any paracetamol for the pain, which they had. I ordered a whiskey to help the tablets go down and loosened my belt and undid the top button on my jeans, which considerably helped to ease the pain. I now felt better prepared for the task ahead.

It was game on! Don took a quick bite of his sandwich and said ready. He was sitting on my left, Mick was across the table. We both had our hands hovering over the pint mugs, like two spaghetti gunfighters staring each other out.

Don had his left arm out looking at his watch whilst his toasted sandwich was in his right hand and was so close to me it was making me feel really queasy.

You could feel the tension, and then Don said, "Go."

Both Mick and I tipped the beer down our throats and slammed our empty glasses down simultaneously on the table, exactly five seconds each.

Don declared it a draw, and as he did so I felt the whole lot plus more surging upwards, and as I stood up it erupted from my mouth all over Don's hand holding his sandwich. It was the fact that I was dead sober in plush surroundings filled with lots of shocked holidaymakers which embarrassed me the most. The looks on the faces of the disgusted customers remains with me to this day.

I never had long to dwell on the situation though, as I felt the second eruption about to explode on to the scene, so knocking over a few chairs I headed for the door as fast as I could.

I had just managed to make it to the door, pushing past incoming customers, and as the door slammed shut behind me, I leant forward with my head in my arms up against the wall so as not to be sick on my shoes. Up it came, just at the moment my jeans travelled downwards. It was impossible to stop or to take evasive action. The ejected contents of my stomach filled my open jeans. It was only then that I became aware of a mass of people passing by, who had just disembarked from the ferry.

This was my greatest embarrassing moment, and there have been more, but this was by far the worse one, especially as I was stone cold sober. I do feel for the Jersey tourist board whose good work in promoting the tourist industry was suddenly wiped out by their visitors' first impression on arrival of a beautiful island.

During this time, when I wasn't at work, Sandy was constantly by my side. He was constantly trying to persuade me to travel abroad, mainly to India and beyond and share an adventure with him.

Sandy was the most important focal point to my suspicious mind in years to come. It was the only part of my story which could be checked with any validity. I must say I was very tempted to leave my friends, but before any decision could be made a tragic accident changed everything.

My pre-booked summer holidays were about to start the following week. I decided to look in the local paper to see if with my limited means, I could afford to hire a car. I was pleased to see that there was one hire company, which had rates as equal to that of Jersey car hire firms, and was based in Weymouth. This would mean that I needn't look into hiring locally and even more importantly, I would not have to pay the each way transit charge for the vehicle.

When Sandy knew of my plans, he wanted to come along, even though he accepted that we would be roughing it sleeping on the floors in mates' houses.

I was pleased Sandy was coming along and was looking forward to his company.

We docked in Weymouth, but found it difficult at first to locate the garage. Eventually we found the location in a back street and it appeared to be very run down. What really shook us was the car which they drove out for us. It was an old Vauxhall Victor about well over ten years old. A real rust bucket. It was obvious that they weren't very professional. You could be forgiven for thinking that they were extras off the film *Deliverance.*

I realised that I could offer them a more lucrative deposit for the car hire than money which would free up extra cash for the holiday, and that was by offering my late father's solid silver pocket watch. They readily accepted.

It must be remembered that it's not unusual for someone like me who was homeless to always take their most valuable possessions with them if they left their temporary base, for whatever reason, purely for safe keeping and security if needed.

# Chapter 18
## Trip Back Home

Both Sandy and I started our road trip back to Redditch full of hope and anticipation. Me because of the chance to see my mother and some old friends that I had missed the past year. Sandy because he was looking forward to meeting the same people that I had missed.

On the drive back up it wasn't long before the old car started giving us problems. Firstly, the windscreen wipers got increasingly noisy until they eventually gave up the ghost altogether. The second problem arose when we stopped at a roadside café for a break. All was well until we came to leave and Sandy opened the back door to get something out of his rucksack, but when he came to shut the door it wouldn't stay shut. We found a piece of wood and jammed it between the door armrest and the floor sill. As we drove back on the road we were discussing the piece of junk we had just hired. It was then that Sandy informed me about the tyres, and the lack of tread on them. We just crossed our fingers and hoped that the badly worn rubber on the wheels would hold out for the journey.

We managed to reach our destination without further problems, but decided not to use the car unnecessarily whilst we were in Redditch.

We had some great nights partying with old friends, but Sandy needed to top up his supply of marijuana. Luckily, the same old suppliers were still around and I managed to fulfil his needs. I was never a user, though I did dabble on rare occasions. I also learned that Seamus had set up selling all sorts of drugs on his return from Jersey, in fact rumour had it that he was one of the main drug suppliers in Birmingham.

The only glitch to my return home was encountering one of my greatest adversaries.

His name was Gerald and he was one of those people who, once drunk, wanted to fight the world, and me especially. Reason being, he had had a long term relationship with a very attractive girl that I had worked with during my time at Terry's Springs. We were close friends, but she was just one of our group that used to enjoy many a night out partying together. What I never knew was that during this period she had tried to break with him many times because of his abusive behaviour. Unfortunately, she had made up a story that she had met someone new. Me!

His uncontrollable aggression in society was well known, but when he'd had a drink, he felt no physical pain. Many times he had started something in a pub, and with my friends' intervention, he was taught many a lesson. But he always came back eventually for more, it was like he had a death wish. The rejection by his girlfriend had really unhinged him.

Early on during our visit back to my home town, Sandy and I were out in one of the town's most popular meeting places, The Unicorn, locally known as the Pig.

In came Gerald, and I wondered if his temper had improved. He had obviously had a lot to drink, and although there had been no contact between us in a year or so, I was on my guard and ready for trouble. He turned from the bar and across the crowded pub he spotted me, and without any hesitation he pushed through the crowd. He put his drink down on our table and started mouthing off at me. He had not improved in any way, if anything he was worse

Before I had a chance to react, Sandy stood between us, turned his head to me and quietly said, "Stay here." He ushered Gerald out of the bar, turning down the corridor towards the toilets.

I quickly followed. I was certain that Sandy could handle himself in most conditions, but did he know he was dealing with an irrational lunatic?

By the time that I got to the doorway and peered down the corridor, I couldn't see them as there was a gang of thirsty revellers coming up the stairs. I assumed that they had gone down the stairs and outside.

When I had pushed past the crowd of people, I spotted them right down the long corridor, past the toilets. Sandy had Gerald around the throat, and being a good six inches taller, had lifted him off the ground. From the distance it just looked like he was giving him a talking to. Being afraid that the situation might escalate, I closed in on them as quickly as I could, but when I got into a few feet of them, Sandy whipped his head round and the look on his face really scared me as I had never seen him like this before. In fact I would not have thought he was capable of being aggressive. He snapped at me to go back, but it came out in such a threatening way that it stopped me in my tracks, and without a second thought, I turned and went back into the bar.

In a very short space of time Sandy came back, sat down as though nothing had happened and picked up his drink. The whole episode couldn't have lasted more than five minutes. Sandy's demeanour sent a chill down my spine and I felt that I never knew him as well as I thought. Gerald came back into the bar and didn't even steal a glance in our direction.

Whatever happened or was said had a profound effect on my old adversary. From that moment on until now, many years later, he has stayed clear of me as if I never existed. Sandy must have put the fear of God into him, much more than me and my mates could ever have done over the previous years. He never ever got in my face again or ever came near.

Our break was coming to an end. We had to be back in Weymouth by Sunday dinnertime to catch the night ferry back to Jersey, but I had promised to stay at my mate Kevin's in Northfield, which is an area in South Birmingham, before travelling back.

I refer to the next incident purely because it had a relevance to something which happened months later.

I felt sorry for Kevin and his lifestyle because he had been working at the Austin Rover plant from the day he left school and had never known another job. His wages were great, well above the national norm, but as each year passed he hated his job more and more. He felt trapped by his high wage and knew that he could never get close to equalling it anywhere else. Kev took us around the livelier pubs in the area, and all in all we had a great night. When we got back to his bachelor pad, Sandy and

I were to sleep in our sleeping bags on the floor. We'd had a fair bit to drink that night and kipping on the floor caused no problem; we were soon in the land of nod.

Problem was that when I awoke the next day I found my sleeping bag soaking wet, even my chest and arms were wet. I felt embarrassed and never mentioned it to Sandy or Kevin. I had never been a bed wetter even as a child.

I rolled my bag up as if there was nothing untoward, had a shower, a quick bite to eat and we were ready to roll.

Months later Kevin came to Jersey on a reciprocal visit, and was to sleep on the floor in his sleeping bag at my and Don's place in Gloucester Street. After the first night out, we had all gone to bed. In the early hours of the morning I dreamt that I was in the sea waiting to be rescued, then I woke up and realised that I was soaking wet. In the dim light I could see Kevin pissing on me. I shouted at him and shot out off of my soaking wet bed. He slipped his John Thomas into his Y fronts and got back into his sleeping bag without even waking. In one way I was relieved that I never wet myself back in Birmingham. I was more perturbed by the psychological reason for him doing it to me, his best mate.

Very early that Saturday morning we set out. We had planned to sleep in Weymouth that night and take the car back before dinner on the Sunday.

Dawn was just breaking and it was only then that I realised we had no lights on the car. As it would be daylight within half an hour we decided to risk it. We had a long drive ahead of us, as it must be remembered the M5 motorway was only half built and never went past Worcester at that point in time.

Disaster struck a couple of miles out of Northfield on the A38, the main road southbound.

There is a small roundabout at the bottom of a short but steep hill on the border of the Lickey Hills. There were no cars about that early in the day, luckily for me, as when I put the brakes on, the pedal slowly went to the floor. I could feel the fluid emptying as the foot pedal traversed downwards.

It was fortunate that my experience earlier on in Jersey of driving without brakes had given me the confidence to rise to the challenge.

We were soon on the M5 heading south. I had to stay focused on the traffic ahead and keep an appropriate distance from the vehicle in front in case I needed to stop. Using the gears as my only means of slowing down, we made decent progress, better than expected.

All went well, even when we left the motorway and continued our journey on the A38; in fact I was pleasantly surprised at how easy it was. My only concern was would the handbrake cable hold out long enough and not wear out or snap during our journey. So far so good.

By the time we reached Taunton we were worried that we wouldn't make it to Weymouth before nightfall, and not having any lights, we felt it would be better to look for a suitable place to pull over before the failing light turned to darkness. Also, it meant that we had now left the relatively safe A38 road which was now some miles behind us, and the minor roads which we were on were far more dangerous to navigate without brakes let alone proper lighting.

We found what looked like a perfect spot, off road, at the tiny village of Crewekerne in Somerset, some forty odd miles from our destination, Weymouth. We settled down to get some sleep. We were both mentally exhausted due to the stress of having to be hyper alert during our drive.

I have no recollection of the time factor for what was to happen next, but can only recount the order of the sequence of events.

All I knew was that it was dark and I was awakened by an unusual cracking noise, somebody shouting, and then a flashlight being shone in my face.

I realised, once awake, that the noise I heard was the back door being pulled open and the piece of wood holding it partly shut was torn from the panelling, destroying it in the process.

It was the Police. Sandy was already being questioned by one of the officers as I alighted from the front of the car. Thank God Sandy never admitted that we had brake problems. However, he said that we had pulled over because our lights had failed. The other policeman looked over the old car and said he didn't believe that the car was hired as what sort of garage would rent out a car with bald tyres. I produced my hire agreement, which he looked at with the help of his torch. He then said that he was taking us back to the police station to check our story out.

They took down all our details, present address and so on, and sat us down in the small hallway in front of the duty desk, which was manned by a young looking constable.

After a short while I looked up to see a uniformed sergant and a plain clothes officer approaching. As they were about to pass the bench where we were sitting, the uniformed officer suddenly stopped in front of Sandy, and said, "Your name is Cooper, you look familiar. Are you any relation to our Reverend Cooper in the village?"

Sandy said, "Yes, I'm his son."

There was a bit of small talk such as he, the policeman said he hadn't seen his father for a while, etc., etc. He then invited Sandy into the office for a catch up chat.

After a while they both emerged. The sergant then said to me, "We are not very happy that a firm could possibly hire out such a car in that sort of condition. We have tried ringing them but there is no answer. It must be just a garage. We will try and make contact throughout the night. In the meantime, one of my officers will take you back to that piece of junk that you're driving where you can spend the rest of the night. Under no circumstances will you be allowed to move it until you get roadworthy tyres put on it."

"OK," we said, and we were taken back to the old car.

I felt so relieved at not having to spend the night in the nick.

We sat there and talked for quite a while. Sandy surprised me when he told me that his parents, who lived locally, had fallen out with him because of his lifestyle. He also had never mentioned that he had siblings who lived close by.

My thoughts turned to getting my father's silver watch back, which I had left as a deposit. Sandy suggested we wait a while, in case we were being watched, and then make a dash for it, taking advantage of the early morning light. Also it being a Sunday the roads would be deserted. With trepidation we set out and made surprisingly good time. I expected to see a panda car at every junction, or even a road block, but no.

I then reasoned that we would be greeted by the police once we arrived at the hire company. At the very least they would

145

have contacted the garage owner. What would happen then? We arrived at the garage at about ten o'clock and waited. Not long after, the owner came bouncing down the road as though he hadn't a care in the world. He greeted us with a smile and handed my dad's watch over. I gave him the car keys, just as he asked, "Did we have any problems?" Obviously the police had not been in touch with him.

I bid him farewell, and we briskly set off down the road. When I was about twenty yards away I turned, but carried on moving down the road and shouted out, "By the way the wipers don't work."

"That's OK," he shouted back.

Sandy then called out, "Problems with the breaks too." Another "OK."

"The back door doesn't shut." Silence. Then Sandy screamed out, "The police say they will be in touch because the lights don't work." At that we fell about, laughing and running at the same time.

We went for a Sunday lunch, and got absolutely blotto, brought on by the sheer relief of making it back to the ferry on time.

Years later when I looked back on this episode lots of questions flooded in to my brain, such as:

Why didn't the police, once they knew we had fled the scene, contact the Weymouth police and inform them of where we were and which garage we were headed to?

They knew we were trying to connect with the Jersey ferry, so why didn't they try to stop us boarding?

They had our address, so why didn't the Jersey police follow the case up?

I would have thought that Sandy might have mentioned his family living in the area long before we parked up off the road.

I had to empty my pockets before being interviewed by the police in Crewkerne, and I would assume that Sandy went through the same procedure. How come they never picked up on the weed that he always carried with him?

Surely the hire firm would have sought recompense for returning their vehicle in such a state.

It was decades later, after reiterating some of these events to a good many of my friends, that a number of them questioned certain events and indicated that they may be linked. My problem was how I could verify any of it.

It was then that my good wife suggested that the Sandy Cooper issue could be investigated up to a point. If we could check that there never was a Reverend Cooper holding a ministerial position in the village of Crewekerne, or surrounding area, then this would show that the police involvement at that time was a complete farce.

My wife and I took our mobile caravan down to Somerset one summer break and could find nothing to establish the fact that Sandy had relatives in the area.

# Chapter 19
# HRH

We never heard any more about the Weymouth fiasco and I really enjoyed my time with Sandy. Little did I know then that I would be losing him as a friend and companion in the not too distant future. Perhaps it was fate, as after spending time with him one to one, I was now being swayed into upping sticks and travelling to Asia with him.

Not long after our little adventure, John brought letters round to our digs, one of which was from the Ministry of Defence. It was a really snotty letter. Its gist was to inform me that it was a condition of being a paid reservist that I was not allowed to reside outside the British Isles without prior permission. What concerned me the most were the forms that I needed to fill in to obtain that permission. There was a strict demand that the forms should be filled in and returned by a certain date. Unfortunately, John never got the letter to me on time, so I was about three weeks after the deadline date.

I could see another conflict between me and the Army in the offing.

I only mention this blip to excuse what happened the next day and what state of mind I was in. Rebellious wasn't a strong enough a word!

Princess Anne was reported in the local papers to be visiting the island the next day. This wasn't a State visit, but was to accept the patronage of the local zoo I think.

The island was getting ready with buntings and flowers. For my part, I was glad to be working away from the hustle and bustle which was going on in and around St Helier.

John had sent word to me that I had more mail and one letter was again from the Ministry of Defence. I felt so down and could see that my time on the island was about to come to an end. I was on the early shift, which meant that I finished at the sewage board at 2 pm.

I decided that because of all the crowds, which not only could I hear, but could see when walking back that instead of going to Gloucester street to change, I would go straight to John and Margret's for my mail. This meant travelling through the back streets of St Helier. It was a lovely sunny day, more like a Sunday with the streets being so quiet.

I had nearly reached my destination when out of one of the many back streets a big black car, decorated with Jersey plaques and flags, turned into my street a few metres in front of me. There wasn't a single soul around as the car slowly approached me. Apart from the driver I noticed there was a lone passenger in the back seat. As it drew level, I guess my frustration with the establishment overcame me.

Princess Anne had probably had an amazing day with the reception of the townsfolk, and giving the royal wave must have come naturally at that moment, accompanied with a beautiful radiant smile and all just for me.

What did I do in return? Give her a big two finger salute and mouthed some obscenity.

The change in her demeanour was immediate and from that day to this I can remember it. It was a look of sheer horror, but even more of total bewilderment.

By the time I turned the corner I was already feeling disgusted and ashamed of myself. I had always felt great respect for the Queen and her family, and I couldn't believe what I had done.

Over the years I felt more and more guilt. The older I got the more often I kept recapturing the image of hurt on her face. I realised that the only way of exorcising these demons was to apologise.

Perhaps because it was the Diamond Jubilee year, I thought that this would be an appropriate time to try to make amends. So in 2012, I wrote to Her Highness asking forgiveness for my actions at that time. I never expected a response, but if I did get a reply I didn't think that there would be any acknowledgement of the incident.

I would have expected that the memory would have been long gone. It has to be remembered that she was a young girl in her early twenties, and most likely this would have been one of her first solo engagements. For that reason alone she may have recalled the event. To go from sheer enjoyment to complete horror in a split second would affect most people.

I did receive a reply from her secretary, and the phrase 'doesn't remember the incident,' which I expected, wasn't forthcoming. The reply was warming, and thanked me for my concern. This left me with the feeling that she did in fact recollect the day in question.

At least I have washed my guilt away over the affair, and since my apology I am no longer plagued with remorse.

# Chapter 20
## Sandy's Disappearance

Like Paul and Eugene before him, Sandy's departure was as swift and as sudden.

We as a group were to go through a traumatic phase, which was to have a dramatic impact on our idyllic lifestyle on the island.

As I have said before, out tightknit group of about a dozen, which included at times some of the staff from the West Hill hotel, was also intertwined with two other groups, which were about the same size as ours. One group were a bunch of lads from Liverpool and Yorkshire, the other group was made up of nurses from the hospital, all from various parts of Britain.

I suppose we all got to know each other from having the same local, the Adelphi pub in Gloucester street, opposite the nurses' quarters.

Life was great, just one big party. Then one night we were all in the pub, with the exception of the northern lads, when the terrible news broke. It was getting close to closing time when two of the northern lads entered with glum faces, and informed us that one of their friends was found drowned after going for a midnight swim the previous evening. He was a very popular member to all of us, and had become engaged just a few weeks earlier to one of the nurses. Apparently they'd had a lovers tiff, after which he had stormed off in a drunken rage. You can imagine the effect this had on all of us, especially on the nurses.

Within a matter of a few weeks most of the nurses had left to return to their home towns and a couple of months later the northern lads group had fractured, and one by one had left the island to seek pastures new. Life was never going to be the same again.

The only lift we had as a group was when Sandy turned up one Saturday morning in an old Bedford van. This meant that we could go further afield for nights out. With Sandy being virtually a non-drinker it meant that we had ourselves a permanent free taxi.

Inevitably, Sandy used the van to try and persuade me to think again about travelling with him to the Middle East and beyond. If we could have all gone together, or even with just Don and Richard, then I am certain that this would have swayed me into going, as long as my two best friends were included.

The weeks dragged on and the sparkle had gone, although we still had the odd good night out on the town.

Most of the time the continentals from the West Hill would come out with us, especially at weekends. All of them were great at chatting up the opposite sex. Two of the waiters were Portuguese, two Italians and one French. Then one fateful night our world was torn apart! We had been on one of our usual Friday night benders and were in high spirits, after the recent tragic events of our comrades. As usual at the end of most evenings, we would call in on a little Italian restaurant renowned for its steaks. It was just off the esplanade, over the road and up a steep hill which overlooked the bay. The esplanade had an adjoining service road where lorries used to leave their unhitched trailers overnight. On this particular night we were approaching the service road in the Bedford van, and as Sandy turned into the road he didn't realise that one of the trailers was double parked. One trailer was at a slight angle and as Sandy swerved to avoid it he collided with another, smashing the windscreen. Had his reactions been slower the outcome would have been more severe, but luckily it was just the front door jamb that took the full force. The impact was enough to send Antonio head first through the windscreen and onto the road ahead. He lay there not moving and covered in blood. We feared the worst but at least he was still breathing. The side of the van was badly damaged and the sliding door was buckled. In those days there were no such things as mobile phones. Sandy, to his credit said that he would drive to the nearest phone box to ring for an ambulance, and then go to the police station to report the accident. The European waiter started to panic and asked for their names to be kept out of it, as most of them were draft dodgers. Sandy offered to drop them off at the hotel after he phoned for an ambulance and before contacting the police. The ambulance arrived quickly but that was the last we ever heard or saw of Sandy. Don and me walked back home to our digs after Antonio was being transported to the local hospital.

We visited Antonio the following day and for many days after, and were shocked at the mess that used to be a very handsome face. He had twenty six stitches in his face alone, apart from his other injuries. A few weeks later, he returned home to Italy. The police never became involved in the incident and we heard no more about it. Sandy was gone forever!

# Chapter 21
## Keith's Return

I have mentioned Keith before. He was the one who followed me to the Alhambra and was the reason we both got caught when we were AWOL. I had warned him not to contact his folks back home, but he did, and we were caught.

I had never seen him since the day we had failed to escape from our escort on Waterloo Station, but we had kept in touch. I have said before, I think, that he looked on me as his hero, like so many others did, because of my rebellion against the Army, although unlike me he was discharged for his sins. He had always suggested that I should look him up should I ever go back to the mainland for a holiday.

With all the trouble and strife Don and me had endured in recent weeks, we were only glad that our two week holiday from the sewage board was just a week away. We thought about a trip to France, but Don talked me into revisiting Redditch. I had already been back home and Don hadn't. After all that was where we had both met and Don wanted the chance to look up some of his old friends.

I thought this would be an opportune time to reengage with Keith, to see how he was going on. The arrangement was to stop off at Bristol on our way back down to spend a couple of hours with him before going on to Weymouth.

I wondered if he was as loopy as he had been back in Bradford. At that time it was crucial for us to have stayed under the radar as far as the police and the authorities were concerned. Which was obvious if one was AWOL. Instead, in Bradford, he used to disappear every Sunday morning, and he would take an air rifle downtown shoot pigeons outside the town hall, which also incorporated the police station. His reason for this was his ambition to be a hit man in the future and he needed to practise. So I was hoping against hope that he had become more level headed. We were to meet him at a certain time in a well-known pub in a dubious part of the city.

Unlike the time with Sandy, we hired a car in Weymouth from a reputable source; it was fairly new and in good working order.

The day finally came when we were to meet up with him. Obviously Don was a bit worried when I reiterated a few stories that me and Keith had been involved in.

We were enjoying our drink in this shady pub when Keith came, all smiles. The minute we bought him a drink, he sipped it, put his glass down and after a few quick words he walked out of the pub. He had been gone so long that we had refilled our glasses.

He came back looking like the cat that had got the cream, with a noticeable glint in his eye. He sat down and asked us if our hire car was a red Mini parked in the pub car park. We said, "Yes."

"Give us the keys," he said.

"Why?" I asked.

He tossed a hundred pounds down on the table and said, "I just sold it for you."

"Sod off," I said or maybe something a bit stronger. He looked just like a puppy that had done a hard trick, but not getting a special reward.

Looking worried he told us he had to get out of Bristol and was hoping to share in the sale of the car. He begged us to take him to Jersey with us. We couldn't refuse as he had worked himself into a right state and had to get out of the city that day.

Don never liked or trusted him after that, but it left me piggy in the middle. Had I known how life was about to pan out, I may have come down on one side or the other instead of sitting on the fence.

At this point in the story I haven't mentioned what an ultra-explosive friendship Don and I had. We seemed to be always fighting. I can't put all the blame on Don, as I knew which buttons to press. However, more than half the time he would just attack me, or anybody else, without warning or justification.

As an example, I remember the time that we picked up these two girls outside one of the discos. We had only just met and it was late, but they agreed to meet us the next night, early on, outside the same disco.

With our testosterone levels at a max, we saw them onto the last bus, and pleased with ourselves for what the next evening might have on offer we started to walk back. I remember strolling up the street, and turning to Don to suggest getting some chips. My next memory was being slapped awake, with a group of women bending over me on the cobbled street. I sat up and looked around, only to see the husbands of the wives who attended me standing over Don, who was cowering up against a wall. He was very distraught and apologetic and couldn't explain why he had attacked me.

I would not say this was a regular occurrence, but it wasn't uncommon. In fact it wasn't always me who was the victim, but being aware of the warning signs made me more defensive.

Our landlady, called 'Lollipop', ran our guest house with her partner of 15 years, and they had a young daughter aged 12. Both Don and I were looked on as a part of their extended family. During the spring/summer months we had to make way for the holiday makers who were staying in the hotel, so we were moved into the attic. This was fine. We stayed out of the way of the paying guests. Our room was a double and decorated to the same well-furnished standard as the rest of the hotel.

We had taken our eye off the ball as far as Keith was concerned, and unknown to us he had bedded our landlady. The first we knew about it was when her long standing partner packed his bags and left. This made Keith in effect our landlord, and the running mistrust between Don and Keith led to a lot of disharmony.

Now, what was about to happen couldn't be laid at Keith's door, but his involvement couldn't have helped. The night everything came to a head, would have seemed very amusing to any onlooker.

Don and I had had a decent night out, and for my part I had to watch what I had to drink as I was due into work at six the next morning.

We had gone into the attic, but I had felt a bit uneasy as Don's demeanour didn't seem quite right. He was sitting on his bed and not making any movement to get undressed.

I decided to get some sleep and undid my belt. This was like a trigger and his mood went darker, so I stopped getting undressed, and he immediately seemed to calm down. We weren't arguing or even talking about anything controversial, but I was becoming more and more uneasy with his mood changes.

Now that he seemed to have calmed down, I carried on getting undressed and I took off my shoes. His mood changed yet again, but my defences were alerted. I started to drop my trousers and he stood up, fists clenched. I pulled up my trousers and he sat back down on the bed, and we continued to talk generally. I remember wondering if this was all in my head as there was no obvious reason for him to be angry.

We both lit a cigarette and I sat on a chair and we talked quite normally, so I got up and undid my trousers again. It was like a starting gun going off. He was off his bed once again, fists clenched. I quickly pulled my jeans back up, and just as quickly he sat down again. By this time I felt very uneasy. *What could I do?* I thought, *Am I just misinterpreting the situation?* I decided that all I could do was drop my jeans but be prepared, just in case.

I dropped my trousers all the way down to my ankles, and his reaction was again instant. Fists clenched he came at me. I had no chance of pulling up my jeans. I ducked the punch he threw, and hit him hard in the face before he could throw another. He fell back on his bed and muttered some sort of apology, blaming the amount of drink that he'd had.

My main concern was the damage my one punch had done. There was a nasty cut on his cheek which was bleeding as well as his nose. I realised that this wasn't going to end here. I needed to leave. I told him that I was going to sleep at work (something I would do from time to time if on the early shift) and let him sleep it off. What happened next, although surreal, I was told was very, very funny.

I quickly got dressed, grabbed my sleeping bag and helmet and got out of the room as fast as possible. I needed to be away

157

before he could look in the mirror and see the extent of his injuries.

The attic stairs were narrow and needed caution to use, especially if in a hurry. The final two flights of stairs were the norm that you would find in any guest house.

I rushed down the first flight, then I heard it. I guessed he had now looked in the mirror. Firstly, there was the cursing and screaming of profanities, and then the sound of a room being smashed to pieces.

I could still hear the commotion when I was outside the hotel. The faster I tried to get away, the more it seemed the Gods were not with me. By the time that I got my pannier open and forced my sleeping bag into it, the outside door was flung open. I never knew it at the time, but apparently Keith had tried to stop Don and find out what was going on. Don, in his rage, had downed him with a single punch at which time Lollipop phoned the police.

Now the funny part, but not for me at the time.

Don's face was full of rage and the blood made it more malevolent. At first he stood in the doorway screaming and threatening, the only thing which separated us was my beloved scooter. He rushed to the front of the machine, I rushed to the back. He then tried to cut me off by switching directions, so I changed directions too. This chase went on for an unbelievable length of time, back and forth, back and forth.

The noise had brought the nurses to their windows, and with every change in direction, the shout went up from the nursing quarters "Ole."

Over the din I heard one nurse's voice scream out, "Kick the fucking bike over."

I had expected this action during the chase. I just hoped Don hadn't heard her.

It must have looked funny because I can remember that the police couldn't hide their amusement when they approached the scene. They tried to calm him, but he kept trying to pass them to get at me. Eventually one of the policemen had him in a head lock. With his struggling I was concerned that he might suffer real damage. The more they applied pressure, the more he struggled. I had to step in and pleaded with the police to let him go as his rage seemed to have subsided. They calmly asked him that if they were to let go of him, would he behave? He said calmly, "Yes."

They released their grip on him. The second they did, he flew in my direction. They only just managed to grab him before he reached me. They had no alternative but to take him away and lock him up for his own safety.

I found out many years later that Don was diagnosed as being epileptic, but he chose not to take any medication. He certainly shouldn't have drunk as much as he did.

The next morning after work, Lollipop said the damage was not that great and she wasn't pressing charges, but we had to get our belongings out within 24 hours. I went to the police station where they asked if I wanted to pursue any charge. They brought Don out and he was back to his 'normal' self.

That was the last I ever saw or heard of Keith. I hope he and Lollipop lived happily ever after.

We were now homeless. Luck was on our side however, at least for a short time. One of the foremen at the sewage board, who knew us and the predicament we were in, came to our rescue.

He offered us a place to stay, free of charge. He had purchased a property which he was renovating, turning it into a guest house. The place had been gutted, but there was water and electrics. The deal was that we could stay there as it suited him that we would act as security, especially as we both worked different shifts. Most of the time one of us would be there at night, sometimes both of us would be staying overnight. What could go possibly wrong?

Don!

# Chapter 22
## Farewell to Jersey

Life was never going to be the same again, and we seriously discussed what to do next. Was it worth trying to rebuild the Utopia that we once had?

We shared the gutted shell of the house with the foreman's little Jack Russell, but we had to make sure he was put outside in the back yard at night. He had a specially made wooden hutch outside the back door. The only thing we needed to buy was a mattress each and sleep on the floor in a designated bedroom.

With the extra money we were saving on rent, we decided to buy a van that we could use to travel through Europe and on to Morocco. So for weeks we searched the ads, looking for a touring van which we could buy.

Our luck was in: we found a van for sale which was the buy of the century.

The story was that there was a garage owner whose son wanted to go travelling abroad when he finished university. The garage owner was nervous about letting his son roam abroad, so he customised an old Interflora delivery vehicle. It had a thorough service, complete with new parts, whether they needed replacing or not. He equipped it with an extra petrol tank and two bunk beds, which could be folded up to give extra space. Fortunately for us, when his son finished university he had met a girl and changed his mind about travelling. His father decided on a quick sale, in case his son had second thoughts. We were over the moon, as it was a lot cheaper than what we had budgeted for.

All we now needed was to wrap up loose ends on the island. Although we had a fair bit saved, we reckoned on saving a bit more then head to Morocco for the winter months like so many of our generation did.

What could possibly go wrong?

When I finished on a late shift at six one morning I was so looking forward to getting some sleep, and was so relieved to get back to our ready-made, albeit, rough home. We always used the back entrance as we were never given keys to the front door.

It was just breaking daylight when I entered the back yard, and what confronted me sent shivers down my spine. There in front of me was a smouldering mattress, which emitted an eerie glow in the half light. What frightened me was that was where the dog hutch stood. So where was the dog hutch, or even more worrying, the dog?

I shot up the stairs as fast as my legs would carry me. I raced into the bedroom nearly pulling the door off the hinge. The first thing that hit me was how loudly Don was snoring and he was out cold on my matteress.

I dragged him out of bed before he was even awake, and wanted to know what had happened and where was the dog? He was still half drunk, but told me he had got really wasted the night before and must have fallen asleep with a cigarette in his hand. He said he was lucky to be alive and he had nothing to extinguish the flames with, so he tossed his bedding and mattress out of the window. In his panic it never registered that the dog was down below.

We both went down, calling the dog as we went, but heard nothing. We dragged the smouldering mattress down the yard, which was mainly hot springs, but all that remained was hot ash. No hutch and no dog remains!

We realised the dog must have been cremated. On our return to the room the one thing that we both had noticed was the damage to the wallpaper, skirting board and floor caused by the fire.

Just our luck, it had to be the only room in this shell of a house which had been decorated.

We notified the foreman, who had given us a roof over our head in our time of need. He was down at his local, which is where he always was when not at work. He had a fiery temperament like most of the Irish I have known. We waited in his local very early that morning as we reasoned that it would be better to inform him of our sins before he started drinking.

When he eventually arrived, and before he had time to order his first pint, Don shot up to the bar and got him his first drink. By the look on his face we knew something was not right, and before we could confess to what had happened, he told us that he had called in at the house earlier and when he saw the remains of the dog house, he hit a new low. Then he heard a dog whimpering. It was coming from beneath the house. He called the dog's name and was so relieved to see his canine friend come scampering out from under the base of the building, quivering but otherwise all right.

We ended up having a long drinking session, and although it was understood that he wouldn't be able to trust us again, there would be no more said about the incident if we redecorated the room. We were relieved, but again homeless.

We stuck to our agreement and repainted and wallpapered within a week.

We slept in our van, which we nicknamed 'Bessie,' and washed and showered at the sewage board.

We had heard on the community grapevine that some of our peers had left the island and had travelled to Munich to find casual work at the Olympics, as there were plenty of jobs to be had. After that there was the *Oktoberfest,* 'Munich Beer Festival', at the end of September.

This seemed an opportunity not to miss. If we were ever going to move on, this seemed like fate.

We both handed in our notice to leave, and Richard, who was still working in the *Europa* hotel, asked if he could join us. We didn't need to think twice, so now there were three of us. Over the next few years we were likened to the trio from the TV series *Last of the Summer Wine.* Richard would be Foggy, I would be Clegg, and Don would, without a doubt, be Compo.

I did say that although Don and I had a very volatile friendship, it wasn't always his fault. I have to share the blame too. This incident in our last week was wholly my fault, brought about again through the excess of drink.

Our mobile home was parked for the last week of our stay, close to our local, the *Adelphi.* In fact we had parked opposite the pub, a short walk across a public green.

On this night in question we had been out for a drink or two. The night was nothing special, or so I thought. We had ended it rather early on, and when we got back to Bessie, Don had stripped down to his underpants and slipped into his sleeping bag. I had just started to undress, and as I was about to take my jeans off I asked him if everything was all right as he was unusually quiet. He responded by saying, in a petulant manner, "It's my birthday today, and I was hoping we could have done something different."

I felt so guilty, as I never knew. He hadn't mentioned it in the days before. What followed was probably the biggest argument that we had ever had.

I insisted that he got dressed and there would still be time to hit one of the many discos or I would treat him to a slap up meal at a place of his choice. The more we argued the more petulant his mood became and this made me even more angry. He refused to budge, so in frustration I dragged him out of his sleeping bag. I remember shouting, "You WILL enjoy yourself."

He was completely out of his bag now, and we both were fighting with such ferocity, which is hard to comprehend in such a small space. During this melee I suddenly thought, *How could you possibly force someone to enjoy themselves? This is ridiculous, this is his birthday.*

I withdrew from the affray, and quickly exited Bessie through the back doors and headed across the busy green to the *Adelphi,* doing my jeans up as I went and tucking my shirt in. I could hear Don screaming behind me saying over and over, "You won't get away with this."

I looked back, still adjusting my clothes, and there was Don outside the open back doors, screaming and shouting with a frying pan in his hand, wearing just his Y fronts. I looked at the faces of the passers-by and wondered what the hell they must thinking.

Don's birthday fiasco was put behind us after he had sobered up the next morning. Now we needed to plan our exit and future journey to Munich.

The three of us had put by enough money to enable us to survive the winter months in Morocco. It was imperative to be earning as much as possible to boost our funds for the months ahead not only to cover our travelling expenses of getting to Munich, but to add a fair bit more to ensure we had the basic comforts. We decided to pool our resources and live as frugally as possible until we could replenish our kitty.

We said goodbye to all our old friends and hoped we would see them again in the not too distant future. In reality this wasn't to be as our reunion came nearly thirty years later on my 50th birthday in Blackpool, where we all came together once more.

# Chapter 23
## Munich

On the morning of our departure Don dropped a bombshell as we were loading our belongings into Bessie. He told us that he needed to go back home to Plymouth for a couple of days to see his brothers who he hadn't seen for nearly ten years.

He was genuinely distraught, and he gave me and Rich a third of his money, which was to help with travel costs with a good bit left over. Most of his belongings were packed on the van, and the plan was that me and Rich would hopefully get a job at the beer festival and wait until the next weekend for Don to hitchhike to Bavaria and meet us in a spot that we deemed suitable at a certain time on a certain day. He wouldn't need the bulk of his money, but would keep it in case he had an emergency, then what he had left when we next met up would be added to our kitty.

Now if you have not travelled on the road as a free spirit, or in a hippy mode, then you may wonder how people who are travelling abroad in different countries can keep in touch with each other when they don't have a stable address.

The answer is 'Post Restante'. All you need to know is in which city or town the person is, or will be, on a certain day or week. Then you send a letter Post Restante to that town or city, and the addressee, on producing their passport, can pick up any mail sent to them at the main post office.

Some friends on the island suggested that we to take items with us which would be easy to sell just in case we got into financial trouble. Some of the best advice that I was ever given. Our one concern was that Bessie had developed a slight fault. Now and then she wouldn't start with a turn of the ignition switch. With my vehicle training the fault was easy to find: it was the solenoid. It wasn't worth the wait to fix it properly, and anyway it almost made it thief proof. It just meant that if the ignition switch failed then all one had to do was reach under the driver's side wheel arch and push the starter motor button. Messy, but it worked.

After travelling to St Malo in France, we travelled eastward to Paris at a relatively steady speed as it was early September and the Beer Festival wasn't until the last two weeks of the month, and we had only 800 miles to travel.

As we had left later than we wished, it meant that when we were close to the outskirts of Paris, daylight was failing. So we were looking for a suitable place to pull over.

We spotted a road up ahead which looked ideal, so I turned into it. The road was very well kept and was unusually straight and long, disappearing in the darkness ahead. After going along for a while, I pulled over on the grass. It looked perfect, away from the main road and quiet.

We got our heads down early and both slept well. When I awoke, I felt the call of nature, and I exited the back doors of the van carrying toilet paper and a small spade. It was misty. Closing the doors carefully so as not to wake Richard up, I headed to the nearby wood, about ten metres away. As I was doing my business, the silence was broken by the noise of a convoy of vehicles; Army vehicles. I quickly finished and rushed back to Bessie. More and more vehicles were passing and I started panicking, thinking that we were on an access road leading to an Army camp.

By the time Rich was awake and ready to go, the mist had lifted somewhat.

What we could just make out in the distance was what looked like a massive building. Whether we were right or wrong we thought we had parked on the entrance road to Versailles Palace. If we had, it was strange that we were ignored by the security. We were soon out of there and on our way to Paris.

We had a fair amount of money between us, but our resources took a hit on the night we arrived in Paris. We had parked up in what looked to be a lively quarter, with a good few bars to explore. Our concern was should we travel too far and get too disoriented through drink, would we find our way

166

back? Richard pointed out that a long way down the end of the street was the Arc de' Triomph, so as long as we could find that monument we should easily find our way back.

After we finished drinking we went in search of the monument with no luck. We waved a taxi down and he took us there, but we couldn't find a street even faintly resembling the street we were looking for.

Eventually we found a taxi rank and someone who could speak English.

We explained our problem and were shocked to be told that there were numerous smaller Arches built around the monument and it could be any one of these. So started a search by taxi, which took what seemed like hours and a chunk of money, after which he dropped us off where he had picked us up. It was now early morning and most places were either shut or closing, but we came across one café which was fairly packed with people and decided to take a break before we resumed our search.

Our luck changed when we got talking to a local man, who was very pro English, and there aren't many in Paris. He listened to our predicament, and after getting a few pointers as to where we had been drinking that night, he was fairly certain as to Bessie's location and offered us a lift to the road he believed we had started our night out in.

He knocked back his drink and we walked out onto the street and around a corner.

He walked up to this lorry, not long in length, but high and bulky. He got in, then said, "Jump up." What followed was one of the most hair raising rides I have ever had.

He hadn't appeared drunk earlier on, but once behind the wheel, he turned from Jekyll into Hyde. Most of the streets were very narrow by British standards and most of them had cars parked on both sides. He drove at speed, as though there were no hazards to be concerned about. Richard and I still argue about how many vehicles he hit during our relatively short journey. The wonder was that there were not any major collisions, just wing mirrors and the odd bumper

Eventually we located Bessie. We had already made up our bunks before tripping the light fantastic, so when we landed back, we were soon out of it.

We were awoken late the next morning by the heavy traffic and noise of the Parisians going about their business.

We set out after finding a café for a bite to eat, and the next port of call on our journey was the city of Strasbourg, on the French German border, travelling through Metz.

On reaching the medieval city, Richard was driving and accidentally stalled the engine crossing the lights on a main city intersection.

No problem except that the ignition failed. Sods law! It had to be in the most inconvenient place possible. I quickly sprang into action, and avoiding the cars passing us on both sides, I fumbled, trying to find the button underneath. All of a sudden Richard screamed out, "Be quick, there's a tram coming!"

I looked up only to realise that we were stranded in the middle of the intersection, with all the other cars gone. It was just us, and we were stuck across tram lines. The tram was heading straight for us, and either he hadn't seen us or just didn't care. Instead of slowing down it seemed to be speeding up. In my panic, I fumbled some more. Then with relief I hit the button, but we both thought at that moment it would be too late. The engine burst into life, and no sooner had it started, Richard realising I would not have time to get on board, sprinted forward out of the way of the oncoming tram. It missed us by feet not yards, but still never slowed down. I have nightmares about it to this day.

We had a restful, uneventful night in the city, and after a brief sightseeing tour on foot, we were soon back on the road again and made good time travelling via Stuttgart.

Arriving in Munich was a great relief, and our main objective was to look for somewhere to park which looked secure, free and close to the city centre.

We found a perfect spot in a large quiet car park, where we thought we would be safe and unobtrusive. More importantly with little chance of falling foul of the authorities. It was the next morning that we realised we had parked up on the Lowenbrau brewery visitors car park.

On our first day we were devastated to find out that we had missed the Oktoberfest altogether. Usually it took place at the end of September each year, but this year the organisers had brought it forward to coincide with the end of that year's Olympics.

Now we needed to find employment and wait for Don to turn up with his money to add to our depleted funds. We had sent word to Don, via Post Restante in Plymouth, his hometown, telling him of our woes and encouraging him to get here as soon as possible. Also, I begged him to bring a packet of Weetabix with him as I had developed a craving for some. We waited a couple of days before we had a reply, and yes, he would bring with him what I had requested.

All we could do was visit the bars that people like us would frequent, hoping to pick up advice as to where to look for work. One day we took a short trip to the World War 2 German concentration camp at Dachau. This is worth a visit by anyone sightseeing this part of Europe; very eerie, not at all like Belsen.

During our trips around the bars looking for work contacts, we took a break and visited what claimed to be the largest beer Keller in Germany, probably in Europe.

Before I tell the story of what happened, I need to explain a little of Richards personality. He was very quiet, clever, conservative and definitely non argumentative.

As we went into the main hall, we were surprised at how many people were sitting at the tables, especially as it was during the day. The place is reputed to hold several thousand people when full. It certainly looked filled to capacity. Directly in front and slightly to our left was a raised stage, where the Oompah Band was sitting, dressed in Bavarian style.

We were about to turn around and leave and come back another day when it was less packed when, suddenly, Rich spotted some vacant seats. I looked to where he was pointing, and at the far end of the room was a table with empty benches. As we neared the table, I was sure that the room became less and less noisy.

When we were within a few metres I noticed a little man dressed in full lederhosen gear, feather in hat, the full works.

My immediate reaction was to think that the table must be reserved for the band. I also noticed that a few of the serving ladies were following our progression to our table. I indicated

169

to them if was it OK to sit there. They all nodded with the same unusual, or should I say, guarded smile.

We sat down, Rich directly opposite this lonely old man, and me sitting to Rich's right. We ordered our steins of beer and both began getting in the mood, enjoying the music.

All was well until our second round of beers came. I was aware that during the time we were in there, people around kept looking over at us

Then it started! The little old man broke his silence, and started talking in German to Richard. Rich responded politely that we didn't understand Deutsch. This really set him off. He started shouting and screaming at Rich, and not once did he acknowledge that I was even there. Richard, like no other, did what only *he* could do

He completely ignored him, as though he wasn't there. Rich carried on talking to me as though there was nothing amiss. So I joined in, and as Rich was talking to me, I started talking to the old man. He ignored me, which got my hackles up. I was now raising my voice to match his. Rich calmly kept talking to me and seemed completely oblivious as to the stranger's rants and even mine.

The situation then was notched up a gear or two when he reached across and took a big gulp out of Richard's mug. Rich never blinked an eye while the old man was drinking his beer; he calmly asked me if I wanted another one.

I was still being completely ignored, which had now raised my temper, so I reached across and picked up the strangers stein, and took a long drink. Again, it was as if I didn't exist.

Rich beckoned to one of the waitresses for another round, and by this time there were hundreds, if not thousands of eyes on us, waiting to see what was going to develop.

The waitress we had ordered with came back, with what looked like the manager, who politely said "Please" as he pointed to the exit.

Not wanting any trouble we got up and followed him towards the main door. When we were opposite the stage he pointed to two empty seats on a bench with a group of smiling people about our age. They were Australians travelling through Europe in two vans.

Our luck was in. They were leaving the next morning, and told us where to try for work as they had heard that they were hiring casual labour at the messegelande (exhibition hall).

We went there early the next morning and stood in line with a large group of non-German men, hoping to be taken on for work.

When the time came to pick the workers that they needed for that day, everyone stood in a line. They first picked any German hopefuls, then me and Richard, and next any Australians, followed by Canadians, Americans then finally Turkish.

This sorting procedure was the same every day. The job, unfortunately, was for just 7 days, or until the exhibition stands were erected.

Hopefully, Don would arrive before the work ended. One matter of concern was the weather. The Alpine roads were completely impassable, and the snowfall in the Alps was the worst for many years. We were worried that we would not be able to leave when Don finally arrived.

Our luck was really in. On the last day of work we had gone to the post office and picked up a message that Don would meet us outside the main Rail Station at noon the next day.

Another piece of luck was that it had stopped snowing in the mountains, and the authorities were hoping to open at least one road through the Alps within twenty-four hours.

It was with mixed emotions that we had our reunion with Don. We were glad that he had made it safely hitching his way across Europe, even though he had a scary moment sleeping in a park in Paris. The big disappointment was that he had arrived broke, and he had eaten my Weetabix to sustain himself whilst travelling.

Nevertheless, we went out that night to celebrate and showed Don around the lively bars that we had discovered, including the beer kellers.

That night when we got back to Bessie, Don reclaimed his bunk bed, which was expected, as after all the van was half his, which meant that Rich was on the floor between us.

After a great night out with no problems, Don reverted to type and for no reason took it upon himself to lash out. He hit me with such ferocity in the face as I was trying to sleep that my head was pushed through the glass side window of the van. That night saw me sitting in the open back doorway, and by the help of the street lights Richard carefully picked what glass he could out of my face, especially around my eyes. Don was so distraught at what he had done he was of little help.

# Chapter 24
## Morocco Bound

Richard did a good job of patching me up, and it took all of our persuasion to talk him out of leaving and going back home.

The American broadcast news that morning was that the Alpine road was now open to traffic, which seemed like fate. Our only concern was our severe lack of money. Our only hope was that we would at least reach Spain and maybe find work in one of the tourist towns and then move on from there.

It was magical travelling through the Bavarian Alps, with the road only slightly wet, but edged by huge snow banks on either side. After about two hours of travelling, we stopped in Austria for a short break in a very small hamlet, with just one bar, but inside it was massive. There was only one other occupant who was quietly sitting on a stool at the far end of a very long bar. Don and Rich were sitting down at a table and I was ordering drinks. I noticed a small, well-dressed man in Bavarian attire staring at me with such intensity it was unnerving. With the style of his white hair, and little white Hitler moustache, I really believed that if Adolf was alive it would have been him to a tee.

I was so worried that I didn't bring him to the other two's attention, hoping that they would spot him. We left the bar, and I only brought the subject up once we were on our way. They both hadn't seen him or believed that he even existed. I wished I had pointed him out before we left.

That night we stopped in a car park to cook ourselves a meal on our small cooker. Our diet was nearly always mash out of a tin, beans and corned beef, or sometimes sausages.

After eating, we spent the night in a typical alpine hostel. Big mistake.

It was easier to sleep in the cold van, with a few beers inside you. We sat at a table, and the large log fire made us feel relaxed and happy. An over friendly Tyrolean came over and bought us a beer, then another. He was so friendly and we never gave it a second thought when he suggested having a game of cards. He taught us how to play a game called Mau Mau. The game nowadays is very common in the UK, but under a variety of names. He suggested we play doubles for money. I thought our boat had come in, how could we possibly lose, with one of us playing on his side? Wrong!

He teamed up with Richard, and after a short time Don and I were panicking on how much we had lost. I had never seen Rich the worse for drink, but this night, happy wasn't the word. He was on a roll! He was winning! He wasn't thinking straight. Had he forgotten that our money was pooled? He and his partner were winning a lot, but overall the three of us were being hit hard.

I only wish that I had noticed earlier that the stranger had a finger missing from each hand. Once I realised we were with a card sharp, I insisted on calling it a night. The German Mau Mau cards he was using I put in my pocket, and told him I was keeping them as a souvenir. I still have them to remind me of how stupid we were.

The next morning we had a tally up of how much money was left and we were shocked at just how much we had lost. We weren't even sure if we would have enough for petrol to get to Spain.

On the top of the mountain, we went through a small section of Switzerland and into Northern Italy, being waved through the border by a little man wrapped in a blanket, sitting in what could only be described as a large vertical coffin with a brazier for warmth. He waved us through without getting up from his seat.

We stopped for a break in Milan, by which time one tank was empty, and the second tank was less than half full.

So far in my story I have never strayed from the truth, but I now have had to decide whether to tell the truth, the whole truth, as to what course of action we took next. I am ashamed to say what we did, but I need to tell it, as it was, 'warts and all.'

We realised that we would not be able to make it to the Spanish border unless we acquired more fuel. So we would siphon off petrol whenever the opportunity arose.

As Don couldn't drive, either Richard or I went with him to do the dirty deed, leaving a driver behind the wheel, prepared for a speedy getaway. This we did regularly without too much trouble,

Until one fateful night. It was me who accompanied Don into a driveway, where there were numerous cars. As we were about to rob the second car of some of its fuel, the front door of the house opened, illuminating the drive and a shout rang out in Italian. We bolted, leaving our 25 litre can and tube behind. As we sped away, we saw the angry group shouting and gesturing in the darkness behind us. After a few miles we pulled into a wood, and switched off the lights. We reasoned that they may have got our registration and phoned the police.

We had an uneasy sleep that night. Our only solace after losing our equipment was that we had now acquired one full tank and the other was at least half full.

It was with trepidation that we set out the next day. We left the wood when the main road became busy.

Our next stop was a great little town called Menton. I've never seen a place more hospitable. We were treated to a good meal, together with free wine when we visited a large local tavern, which seemed like an English version of a Social Club.

We set off and headed to the border, which was the crossing point between Italy and Monaco. Just a few miles to go and we would feel safe. We rolled up to the outskirts of Monte Carlo, and were greeted by a road block, manned with a dozen or more police, their cars all lined up off the road.

Our hearts sank when we were waved into a long lay-by; no other vehicles had been stopped. We were not worried about being searched, but was it to do with our fuel stealing? It was about noon. We noticed other cars and lorries were just waved through. We sat there worrying for a good three hours, and then the police cars started leaving the control point at regular intervals. This went on for a good few more hours until there were no police left. We thought we would chance it, thinking that maybe they had forgotten about us. By this time it was dusk and the light was going.

175

We gingerly drove past the point where the control check was, then through the town and on to the border control for France. Richard's reasoning for us being stopped was that because we looked like hippies, they didn't want us to taint the town's reputation. We couldn't think of any other logical reason. We entered the country with no further problems.

As we went into Nice, Rich remembered that he had left his sleeping bag on the roof to give it an airing when we were at the checkpoint. We stopped, looked, but it was gone. We then went shopping around the city to replace it, and to buy another container to collect fuel. This virtually wiped our funds out.

Next we went on to Montpellier, where we collected more fuel. At this point we were really sick to death of our diet, in fact it was affecting our teeth. When we realised our larder was down to our very last couple of snacks, it was no big deal. At least we had water.

We now had two, almost full tanks of petrol, so early the next morning we pushed on to the Spanish border, not stopping at Perpignan as planned.

The relief of crossing into Spain gave us a euphoric feel, but within half an hour we found ourselves at our wits end.

I'm sure we fell afoul of a tourist trap. We were always careful to drive within the law, speed limits and the rest. Those first few miles in Spain were littered with nonsensical road signs. The no overtaking signs and safe to overtake signs seemed to be a hundred yards apart and less. By the time you overtook a vehicle, there would be a counter sign forbidding it.

It was bound to happen! We didn't pull back in quickly enough, and must have only just crossed double white lines by a metre or so. Like a flash, two motorbike police waved us down. They couldn't speak any English at all. They quickly wrote out a speeding ticket for 2,000 pesetas. We pleaded with them, but it was no good. Don had a brainwave and disappeared into the back of Bessie, and brought out a bottle of whiskey. We had just passed an off-road transport café and between the three of us, after a relatively short time, we had managed to convey to the police that we had no money, but if they would allow us to go down to the truck stop, we might be able to sell the whiskey and pay the fine. This they let us do. Rich stayed behind, while Don and I walked down to the restaurant. What happened next disgusted us. This brand of whiskey was not readily available in Spain, unlike today. It was very costly to buy, and out of reach of the average Spanish working man.

We asked loudly if anyone spoke English, and a young couple said that they did.

She was from Newcastle, and he was a Spaniard who had been working in England. They were on their way to meet his family. After listening to our story, he offered us 3,000 pesetas, and said that after paying our fine, the extra would buy us food.

She went ballistic, and argued that we only needed 2K. His argument was that he could easily get 5K for the bottle. He took out the money, and she snatched it from him, and gave us just the 2K we needed for the fine. They argued so fiercely and he looked at her with such disgust that I would bet he was having second thoughts about his future with her.

# Chapter 25
## Journey's End

After paying the fine, we resumed our journey with a bitter taste in our mouths.

That day, we reached our first hope of finding work, in the resort of Lloret de Mar. As we were about to find out, resorts like Lloret were ghost towns during the winter months. The casual workers who help out in bars are long gone.

We thought of selling blood to get some money together, but Richard was very anti the idea. Instead, he insisted on selling his very expensive radio. We knew what this radio meant to him, and tried to dissuade him, but he insisted and said that with what we had been through the past weeks we deserved a bit of respite and regeneration.

Reluctantly we agreed, and with a very heavy heart he went to a shop which advertised the buying of such items. Had it been the summer season then he would have got a lot more for such an expensive piece of equipment. As it was he received a fraction of its worth.

We stayed in the resort for two full days, still hoping that one of us might strike lucky with a job, but still filling our faces with food and our bellies with beer.

We had parked Bessie up on the southern tip of the beach, which was out of the way and out of sight of the authorities.

On our last night we had gone out to enjoy ourselves and ended up in a British bar called the Londoner. There, we befriended one of the barmen, who pushed free shots of Tequila at us all night. We staggered back to Bessie only to find that someone had broken in and stolen anything which might look valuable. We guessed that we had been conned by the friendly barman, who had plied us with drinks all night, but how could we prove it? The power of Karma!

We resumed our journey south taking the coast road as the toll roads hadn't been built at that time. We tried to sustain our meagre diet by taking unripened oranges from the groves that we passed. At least we had one full petrol tank. We found it impossible to steal fuel in Spain because of three main reasons. One, the majority of fuel caps were lockable. Two, we couldn't gain access to the plug at the bottom of the tank to drain the petrol into our plastic wash bowl, as we had been forced to do a couple of times before. The reason was nearly all the cars had a metallic dust shield covering the underside of the car. The last reason was that, the majority of cars were diesel and not petrol.

Later that day we arrived at Spain's largest resort, Benidorm. If we couldn't find work there, we wouldn't find it anywhere. We spent two full days calling in to most of the hotels and bars. It was just the wrong time of the year to find anything.

We were now at the end of our tether, hungry and feeling dejected.

We knew that much further down the coast, at Valencia, one of the major cities, there was a British Consulate. Maybe they could point us to any employment that could be available. So off we set, trying to keep positive.

On arriving in Valencia, instead of heading straight to the consulate we went to the port.

Still filled with hope, we trudged around the port, but no luck. Still not wanting to give up just yet, we decided to do a bit of beachcombing. The beach close to the port was filthy, with oil slicks and discarded rubbish scattered about. We never knew what we were hoping for, maybe anything we could sell or, who knows, a lost wallet with money in it. We were, if nothing else, hopeful.

We walked in a line scouring the sandy wasteland. All of a sudden Don shot forward and dived on to the beach in front of him. Whatever it was he spotted soon went in his mouth and he stood there chewing. Richard's response was to violently throw up. For someone with an empty stomach it was surprising the amount he ejected. To this day Don wouldn't divulge what it was that he had devoured. To be honest I'd really rather not know!

It was this act which made us realise what depths we had sunk to and we had no choice but to seek help.

Off to the consulate we went, with all our hopes pinned on them pointing us in the direction to gainful employment. They were very sympathetic, but couldn't help. They spent a long time trying to convince us to return to the UK under repatriation.

It was quite an easy process. They would give us X amount of money to go back, including the money for petrol, food, ferry and the like. In fact it was all negotiable as it didn't matter how much we were given because we would have to repay it all at a later date to the Home Office. The way it worked was each Passport was stamped '*To be retained by HM Customs on return to Britain*'. To regain your passport you had to pay back, in full, the amount borrowed.

We obviously overestimated the amount of money needed, which meant that we didn't need to rush back to old Blighty. In fact, we took a leisurely trip back, going out each night and drinking local wine where possible. It was the most peaceful two weeks of my life.

We nearly had a major disaster, which led to a massive argument between us. As I said before, the van was owned by Don and me equally. Don couldn't drive, which meant that the driving was shared between Richard and myself. I had driven for a hundred miles up the coast road when we came upon a small holiday resort, which had been boarded up for the winter. The beach looked very inviting, so I pulled off the road and parked just on the edge of the beach. It was a hot sunny day, so I suggested that we cook a meal here, and as I deserved a break, I left them to sort the food out. I grabbed my soap and towel, ran down to the water's edge, leaving my towel on the beach. This is how we washed our clothes, in the sea fully dressed. Then, once we had finished, we would strip off and dry our clothes by hanging them on the van. Anyway, I had finished my ablutions and lay on the beach to relax. I could hear further up the beach Don and Rich having a heated argument, then there was nothing but an uneasy silence.

Next thing I heard was the sound of the van approaching. I looked up and couldn't believe my eyes when I saw Bessie grind to a halt on the soft sand. I was fuming and started on Richard saying he should have had more sense than to drive the van onto the beach. He agreed and said, "Tell that to Don."

Apparently, Don had pulled rank by arguing that he was part owner of the van, and that Rich shouldn't have any say in his decision. Rich, in frustration and to prove a point, drove it down the beach until it finally got stuck in the sand. It took us the rest of the day to salvage our temporary home, using blood, sweat and tears plus bits of wood and anything else we could lay our hands on. God knows what we would have done if we had failed.

On arriving back in England, our first port of call was to my oldest friend and ex-Army mate, Trevor, not forgetting his good wife Brenda. They made coming home a bonus. They fed us and looked after our every need for a few days with remarkable hospitality.

Then, two of us headed back to Redditch, while Don went home for Christmas. When we arrived back in my hometown, we parked up on the grounds of the old council yard, which by coincidence was in George Street, where I grew up. It was just rubble and waste ground, but made me feel at home. Disaster was just around the corner. Each night we would spend our evenings in the Nags Head or Rising Sun, next door. They both had raging coal fires. The Nags had two in each room, and the landlord, Steve, would let us warm ourselves all night without buying a drink. On the second, third and fourth nights, I spotted an old acquaintance enter the pub, along with an afro Caribbean youth. They would look around and quickly disappear. Each time I tried to catch his attention, but we never made eye contact. I thought he didn't recognise me because of my facial hair. I couldn't call it a beard as that would be an insult to beards.

At this point I should relate how I became acquainted with the nightly pub visitor. Let's call him Marcus. We got to know him in the days before our Jersey adventure. He knew that Seamus, Eugene, Brendon and me used to travel to Birmingham every few weeks to have Friday nights out in the Irish quarter. We would travel in by bus and return by taxi.

Marcus came up with a proposition. He would take us in to Brum and bring us back, all free of charge, and he would also stand us a round of drinks.

We weren't stupid, and we knew that it sounded dodgy, but stupidly we went along with it.

The way it worked was that he would drop us off in the Irish quarter, with the understanding that we would be in a certain pub near the theatre at 10.30. He would be there when we arrived, buy us all a drink, and then he would leave. His second and most important condition was that once he left, we would leave 10 minutes after and meet up with him at a preset location, which was always a matter of seconds away.

This ritual went on three times, and each time he always returned within the ten minutes. Then he would put his head around the door, and say, "Right, let's go."

We obeyed the urgency in his voice, and his vehicle was always outside and very close by. We often wondered what he was up to as he never brought any packages back with him. Then one night we bumped into a group of lads who he had previously used to do the same routine with, until they found out what it was all about and they told us the full story.

It went like this. He made a living out of 'rolling queers.' In other words, he would travel to the city to socialise with gay men, and pick out his victims using his Latin looks and smooth manner, but deep down he was a vicious thug. One night he picked up the wrong one, and it didn't go according to plan. The gay bloke fought back and raped him. From then on, he conned people like us to travel with him for protection.

On the fourth night when we got back to Bessie, the back doors had been forced open. My immediate thought was *Marcus!* Not only had they stolen our clothes, but what they didn't want they scattered around the dump of a car park, including birth certificates, photos etc. Worst of all, they had found and taken my only treasured possession, my father's silver pocket watch.

I swore that I would swing for them both when I found them. The next day I went to the Police station, but they weren't interested as they had already been arrested an hour or two before I got there. Apparently, it was for armed robbery on an old lady in her eighties who ran a sweet shop. She died as a result of the attack. I think the young afro Caribbean eventually was sent back to Jamaica after serving his time. In later years, rumour had it, that he returned to be one of the leaders of the Birmingham 'Yardies'.

We realised that as long as we slept in Bessie, we would be a target, so we found lodgings in a working man's guest house. I found work locally and ended up back at a large manufacturing firm where I had worked before. The robbery affected Richard so much that he went back home for Christmas. One of the last things he said to me before leaving was, "I couldn't believe that they even took my underpants."

I said nothing, but felt terrible for days after, wondering why the hell they didn't take mine.

Welcome paranoia!

# Chapter 26
## Butlins

Richard had gone home, but Don came back to Redditch on Christmas Eve.

Not long after we had settled in to our digs, Don, after a good night out, took it upon himself to pick a fight with our landlord. I and the others thought we had calmed him down, and we all started up the stairs to bed. Next thing I knew, I was waking up in hospital. My bottom lip was so badly cut that to this day I still have no feeling in it. Don didn't remember the assault.

We regrouped in the spring at Butlin's Skegness, a job which we had obtained through Richard's efforts.

He had attained the post of assistant manager in one of the main restaurants, but before the season had started, he was promoted to manager. Don and I were given jobs on the fairground. My main job was to be in charge of the train (The Princess Anne) which was a two and a half ton locomotive.

Butlins has changed and evolved over the years, but back in the early '70s it was a frightening place to work. Danger on the rides was pretty, well, universal, but I thank God for health and safety being brought in over the years to make the attractions as safe as possible.

To give some idea of what I mean, the most dangerous attraction was an indoor ride for children, and it was the one ride that no one wanted to operate. The ride was for toddlers, aged two and three years old, and you were on tenterhooks every time you were forced to operate it.

The management had a big problem in trying to persuade the workers into taking on the glass collecting duties during the

Cabaret nights, until the night I was forced into performing these duties.

I realised it had great advantages. Yes, it was hard work collecting glasses during the minor acts, and it was surprising how easy it was to accidentally pick up a customers glass which you thought was finished with. When clearing glasses we each had a four wheeled metal trolley with three shelves. The most important rule of the show was that there would be no collections taking place during the 'Star Act.'

This gave me an idea for a cunning plan (sorry Baldrick).

I approached the management and put forward my proposal, knowing that they would go for it because of their problem in staffing these cabaret nights.

I would guarantee six volunteers for each occasion. Firstly, they would pay us time and a half for the night, and secondly, and most importantly, if there were spare seats available then we could take off our white coats and watch the main event.

This was agreed to, and it worked like a dream. In the run up to the main act, we gathered up various unattended drinks along empty glasses, and put them on the bottom tray of the trolley (this was known as minesweeping).

We would put a staff reserved sign on a table, which was tucked away at the back of the auditorium.

Result! It meant that once a week we had free drinks and watched first class star turns, for which we were paid over the odds for our trouble. I had never thought much of Roy Hudd, until I watched his adult show on a night such as this.

Some time later, I was approached by management to rally my gang of volunteers to help at an upcoming and prestigious event. This involved one of the funniest happenings in my life. We talk about it even now. To appreciate the humour in this next situation will require imagination.

Butlin's were hosting a special equestrian show which, it was rumoured, was being televised on a local station. It had been raining on and off for a whole week preceding the event. In hindsight the gymkhana should have been cancelled.

The camp's security were supposed to have been the assistants on the ground, picking up the fallen poles and reconstructing the fallen fences. Unfortunately for the management, they had gone on strike, or on a work to rule.

Most believed that it was the inclement weather, which was the reason they prolonged their strike action.

They agreed to pay us the security crew's going rate for the day. They stipulated that we must wear the overcoats issued to the security guards which ensured that we looked uniform, at least on the surface. This caused mayhem on the day as the long overcoats were designed for people over six feet in stature. They were of the same design as that of the Royal Guards, both grey and heavy.

For the tallest of us they reached the floor, but for me and most of the others, there was about at least two inches of overhang. To top it, they supplied us with flat caps (officer style), which were at least a size too big. The overall effect made us look like Wombles on a bad day.

We were driven down to the gymkhana arena, which was bordered by steep downward slopes. This was where each group was to hide until we were needed to spring into action. We were split into four groups of four, and stationed around the arena.

The weather was miserable and fluctuated between drizzle and rain, and to a man we wished we hadn't volunteered.

The show started and it was almost straight away that the bedlam began to unfold. It couldn't have been better choreographed, to create such brilliant mayhem. If they had issued us with boots or Wellingtons, then what was about to occur may never have happened.

The first group sprang into action, although not quite the action that was intended. It would have been difficult enough to climb the wet bank in trainers, but when each step taken was on the overcoat that you were wearing, it became an impossibility. However, we had the bright idea that two of us could hoist one team mate up over the brow of the ditch by their ankles then they could roll away to a level part of the arena. This would allow them to come back and help to pull the others up from the gully. This all took time.

Once all four of us were on top of the bank, then you might think that the hard part would be over. No!

Now the real comedy began. It was obvious that none of us could walk or run without holding our overcoats up, like a woman would do, if stepping through a puddle.

186

This wasn't very effective as without being able to use our arms we couldn't keep from slipping over. Forgot to mention the hats. How do you hold your coat up and still keep your balance? It becomes almost impossible when you are blinded by your hat slipping over your eyes. I lost count of how many times someone, blinded by their headgear, bumped into another person thus knocking them off balance. Even worse, with arms flailing, and trying to keep or regain balance, it was inevitable that a forearm smash to the head would down someone too close to them.

Could it become more difficult? Oh yes!

Once we had spotted the other three teams having the same trouble, and seeing how funny they looked made us realise how stupid *we* must look. It became even more difficult to remain upright on the slippery surface when we were laughing so hard. All this activity churned up wet grass turning it into a mud bath.

The laughter from around the arena was deafening. It was now happening in all four corners of the field. The farce seemed to go on forever. Eventually, the powers that be called it a day. I don't think that even one fence was ever reconstructed.

If only it had been videoed!

I could go on all day referring to comedy situations during our spell at the camp, but I will refrain from telling more, except for the next two incidents.

I have said that it wasn't always Don to blame for his violent outbursts when he had drunk too much. I think he felt pent up frustration towards me that would come to the surface when drinking. I found him so easy to wind up, especially early in the mornings. I refer to the next incident.

Our uniform for working on the fairground was a royal blue jacket, trimmed with a canary yellow collar. Nearly all the jackets were well worn and faded. One night I heard a rumour that a certain amount of new jackets had arrived at the store, but I kept the news to myself as they were issuing them on a first come first served basis.

The next morning, I got up early and picked up my brand new jacket before I went for breakfast. The canteen was full of workers, barmen, chalet maids, fairground workers etc., when I waltzed in looking like a mannequin in my new colourful outfit.

The odd wolf whistle soon turned into a crescendo. I picked up a couple of hardboiled eggs and some toast. It was noticeable that Don was the only one that didn't lift his head up, I guessed he was jealous. I sat down opposite him, but he never acknowledged my presence, which really pissed me off.

I chopped the top off my eggs, but they were only half cooked. I told Don how runny my eggs were, but got no response. I knew him well and realised that it was a hell of a hangover he must be suffering from. So, to attract his attention, as his head was bowed eating his cornflakes and his long hair dangling down and dipping into his milk, I did something really stupid. Seemed like a good idea at the time.

I thrust forward both arms, each holding a sloppy egg, and shook them under his nose saying, "Look Don."

His reaction belied someone suffering from a hangover. Quick as a flash he pushed my hands back, spilling both gooey eggs over my newly prized uniform. In anger I threw what was left at him. With eggs dripping from his hair, he retaliated by throwing the remains of his cornflakes at me. Of course in an exchange such as this, there are bound to be innocent bystanders. This then started a small interchange of missiles from unknown sources, which developed into a full blown war, involving the hundred or so breakfast eaters. It was just like a slap stick movie of yesteryear. Both Don and I made a quick exit and stopped outside the door to watch the food fight in progress, until we spotted security arriving, then we legged it.

The next incident was very quick in its action, but became the talk of the camp for the next few days.

After a night out drinking, we of the fairground variety would push or throw each other into one of the outside swimming pools on the way home to our beds. It was just an end to a good night.

One night, Don and I were staggering home when he spotted a lone man sitting by the pool looking very much down and dejected. I was surprised and stunned when Don said, "Let's dunk him in the pool."

I felt sorry for him as he obviously had problems.

Before I could argue Don whispered, "You grab his left arm and Ill grab his right."

We were already up to where he was sitting, so I had little time to think, only to react. I grabbed the strangers arm firmly. Unfortunately, Don didn't act at all.

All I remember is that our target was much stronger than he looked and pulled me round in front of him. His punch took me by surprise, and I felt my back hitting the water. Half dazed, he helped to pull me out. Don was nowhere to be seen. Apparently, we had picked on a semi pro boxer, a nice bloke He was more concerned that I might have had concussion. Never tried that again!

We were to leave Butlins within a couple of weeks because of tax reasons.

# Chapter 27
## My Shame

We had to leave Butlins as we had come to our earning's ceiling. In the '70s, people of our generation could afford to travel, because of the structure of the tax system. The way it worked was, you had to be careful not to earn more than your personal tax allowance before the end of the tax year. Instead, you would leave you job which would be on the books, and then find casual work, until you were ready to travel.

Then you could claim all the tax back as a lump sum, which took about three weeks. What a great saving plan it was.

Don, me and four others left Butlins in our trusty van named Bessie, and we headed to the hop fields in Kent, where we knew there was plenty of work for casual labourers. Richard had decided to stay on at the camp as manager of one of the large restaurants.

There was only one person from here on relevant to my story, and his name was Angus.

Angus was one of these people who, it seemed, was born accident-prone, and supplied us with many a laugh and giggle with some of his antics.

We found work at the first farm we called at, which was Corfe Farm, situated in a small village called Nettleford. The owner, Paul, who it could be said was from the upper class, was one of the most down to earth person I had ever met. It was a pleasure working for him and his family. We planned on staying there until the end of the hop picking season, but as that would have left him with a labour problem, we decided, because of his kindness to us and other workers, that we would stay until the apple picking was over.

It was during this period of my life that a situation arose

that made me feel not only disgusted, but ashamed of myself.

In the first few days of hop picking, I got what I looked upon as a promotion. That was, not working in the fields, but in the Oast house, where the hops are dried. The downside was having to work and sleep in the same vicinity as the drying crop. The upside, was that it was a higher wage and free beer, as much as you wanted, 24/7.

The large family groups from the East End of London did the heavy work. This is how they spent their holidays, and got good wages into the bargain.

One day, the foreman of the farm called me to one side, and asked for a favour.

His problem was that one of the regular farm worker's wife was trying to seduce him. I felt close to the family of the foreman, and the idea that some jealous unhappy wife should try to break his family up, really incensed me.

So under his guidance, I constructed a poison pen letter to the mother of the worker, stating that her daughter in law was cheating on her son.

Our hope was that the unhappy wife would be confronted by the mother in law, and would be taken in hand by her, or at worst be split from her husband for being a potentially cheating wife.

I had to think long and hard about this decision, but it fell into my 'philosophy of life.' That is;

*You can only do as much good as you dare do bad, and only do as much bad as you dare do good.*

Even so, I did have strong reservations before posting the letter.

It was the following weekend when the talk of the farm community was the disappearance of the farm worker's wife. She was last seen going down to the post box in the village, dressed only in her slippers and dressing gown.

More worrying for me, was the disappearance of the foreman at the same time. At first the link was not made, as the foreman, who had gypsy blood in him, often did vanishing acts when the mood took him.

The police were called in, and treated it as a potentially serious crime of abduction. It was nearly a week later that she

191

was returned home by the police.

Yes, she had been abducted on the way to post letters. It was at the hands of the foreman, who it seemed had this uncontrollable desire to be with her. So he had used me to cause a split between a happily married couple. I had never felt so used, or taken advantaged of, as I did then.

The time came when it was the end of the harvesting, and for us to decide whether to give it another go, and to try again to spend the winter in a sunnier climate.

We thought that the Canary Isles seemed the best bet, and made the unwise choice of route via Morocco, instead of thinking of catching a ferry in Spain. On a map it seemed logical to board a ferry at Casablanca. Big mistake!

It was a sad day when Don told me that he wouldn't be going, as he had fallen in love with a young holidaymaker whilst we were at Butlins. He wanted to see if the relationship was going to work out, which it did, as they are now in their 42nd year of marriage. Out of the others, only one wanted to give it a try, and that was Angus.

So with a heavy heart we all said goodbye to each other, and promised to keep in touch.

# Chapter 28
## Canaries Bound

Earlier I described Angus as being very accident prone, and some of the situations that he found himself in kept us all amused many a time back at camp.

It wasn't until we arrived in France the next day after parting with the others that I realised the dark truth behind his many antics. He was nearly blind! It seemed that his long sight was not that bad, his vision was only affected when he tried to distinguish close up objects.

It wasn't long before I realised that he had an even worse trait. He loved to argue!

He would argue about almost anything and everything. I should have turned back then, but I felt he would settle down eventually as time went on. Wrong!

At least we had plenty of money between us, but the only problem was that he hated spending it. I had always been brought up to believe that Yorkshire men were well known for being careful with their money, but he took it to a new level.

On our first day in France, we stopped for the night just outside Paris. We decided to spend the next day exploring the city. Two things happened, which soured my feelings towards the French. We parked up and walked the streets, soaking up the Parisian atmosphere. We found ourselves in the Jewish quarter late in the afternoon.

One of the many clothing stores had people standing outside vying for business. Two men spotted us, and assumed we were American because of the colourful vest that Angus was wearing, which was emblazoned with '*St Louis University*'. The younger of the two men shouted out, "Are you Americans?"

We said "No" and tried to ignore them and walk away. The older of the two directed his next comment to me in broken English, "You British?"

Picking up my walking pace I yelled back, "Yep."

He caught up with us and put his arm around my shoulder, and very politely guided me back to the shop. Then passing by all the clothing on display, he took me inside. All the time he kept repeating himself in his heavy French accent "You British?"

I kept nodding. He was forever taking jackets down off the rails and asking me to try them for size. All I could do was to repeat over and over, "No money."

His reply was always the same, "Free, no money, free."

Eventually, one leather jacket fitted like a glove. So I thought I would go along with it, to see if he was genuine. He took it from me, wrapped it in brown paper, and with his arm back around my shoulders, took me down to the entrance of the shop where the till was situated. He spoke to the young man on the till in French who in turn said to me "So, you're Yiddish?"

"No," I said, "British." He then spoke to the old man in French, who very roughly tore the parcel out of my arms, and started shouting angrily, and virtually pushed me out of the shop. Angus, who had been waiting outside couldn't believe the change in the shop keeper from me entering the shop to being thrown out.

Angus suggested we get a drink, and while I was in the shop he had got into a discussion with a man outside a bar who was trying to entice passers-by into entering with the promise of plenty of girls and a live show.

I tried to tell him that it was a 'clip joint', but he didn't know what I was talking about, but with my experience down in Soho, I knew what we were letting ourselves in for. He couldn't get in there fast enough.

We were greeted by a sexily dressed girl, who insisted that we had to buy her a drink. Even at this point I tried my hardest to persuade him to leave, but I reasoned that in the North of England they didn't understand the concept of these places.

Anyway, a waiter soon came to our table. We were the only ones in there. Then a girl started gyrating on the small stage. So, at this stage, there were me and Angus, and the hostess sitting at a table, a girl prancing around on a small stage and the barman.

The waiter soon brought over two bottles of beer and our hostess declined a drink.

As the waiter removed the top off the beer bottle, I asked him, "How much?"

He responded by saying, "80 francs." I quickly put my hand over the top of the bottle and told him to take mine back, but he said the till had already been rung up, so we had to buy them.

What happened next really unnerved me, especially as Angus, who was a rugby player and bigger in stature than me, started to join in the argument.

The waiter gave him a big backhand slap across his mouth, which seemed like a signal as immediately two men leapt across the bar with bottles in their hands.

I realised the danger of the situation we were in. I quietly said to Angus, "I will keep them talking, and you see if you can sneak outside, as I noticed a couple of Gendarmes nearby, see if you can get them to come in."

I don't know why it worked, but they let Angus leave, while I sat all relaxed in my chair. I asked the hostess if anyone in the club could speak English. She came back with a much older woman who I assumed was maybe the owner. Angus came back in and said the two policemen were still outside, but were indifferent to our situation.

The older lady then negotiated with us as to how much we could afford, and we settled on half and paid 40 francs (in today's money about £40). This didn't please Angus at all. At least it got us out of there. I only recall this story as it had a profound effect on Angus, and he never stopped ranting on about it. He had always been careful with his spending, but after this latest experience he became a complete miser. This caused a big split in our relationship later on, even though we both had plenty of money left.

Apart from his constant arguing at almost everything, I don't remember anything else about our journey south. I just hoped he would put it behind him. That hope was well and truly dashed.

The next 800 or so miles seemed like purgatory, and I seriously thought about turning back. I just kept telling myself that he would get over it. It made me realise the importance of the phrase "It's not where you go, but who you go with."

I really tried not to say anything controversial, but it never worked. Even saying it looked like it was going to be a nice day caused a dispute. I was getting to the end of my patience, and made up my mind that once we reached the Canaries we would have to part company unless his demeanour changed.

The straw that broke the camel's back came when we were in Almeria, in the south of Spain. We were on a road which overlooked a deep valley, and when we looked closer we could see a Wild West replica town.

That night after parking up, I suggested that we have a break and go out for a beer, but Angus was so against it as it would mean spending money. To be honest I was relieved, as I was becoming sick of his habitual arguing and looked forward to having a break from it all.

It was sheer luck that one particular pub I went into had an English owner, and the walls were plastered with signed photographs of film stars.

It turned out that most of the spaghetti westerns were filmed around the valley we had spotted. The owner told me that if we stayed around for a couple of weeks then he was confident that he could swing it for us to get jobs as extras on the forthcoming film.

Filled with this good news, I got back to Bessie, hoping the news would cheer Angus up, but not a chance. He was of the opinion that we would be spending money by frequenting the bar for the next two weeks, and it was against his principles to pay money out in order to get work.

That was it!

I couldn't wait to get to the islands so that we could go our separate ways. The next morning I pushed on with the intention of bringing our partnership to a close as soon as possible.

I had made a very bad decision in going as far south in Spain to find a port to get us across to Morocco and down to Casablanca, which I reasoned to be the nearest port to Fuerteventura as possible.

We had some frightening moments, especially when in Tangier. I could have been mistaken for a local, but Angus with his fair hair looked every bit an Anglophile.

We got lost in the Kasbah, with its narrow streets and menacing looking inhabitants. I admit I was scared, but Angus completely lost it. I had heard the expression 'Blind Panic,' and what I witnessed was the reality of what it means. He was running into walls as if they weren't there and screaming. This brought more and more Arabs out of their homes. They looked bewildered at the scene before them. Luckily, one young Moroccan who spoke fluent English calmly said, "Follow me," and he led us up and out of the dark narrow alleyways.

I decided to get Angus away from Tangier as quick as possible. We made our way back to the van, which was surrounded by a crowd trying to peer inside it. I probably have never felt as helpless as I did at that moment, scary was the only adjective to describe the situation. I pushed past them without making eye contact, and spoke sharply to Angus telling him to get in.

Thank God Bessie fired up first time and I sped away, just driving anywhere hoping to pick up a road sign showing the way to Casablanca. Once we found the right road and had left Tangier behind us, Angus, who had quietened down from his hysterical outburst, informed me that a group of young Arabs packed into a car were following us.

All I could do was ignore them, and after quite a few miles, they stopped and turned back. The relief was enormous.

We drove and didn't stop until we reached the capital, Rabat, and what a relief it was. This city was so alien to the other places in this country. It's very European looking, and we felt safe for the first time. We parked up in a suburban area and had our first night of worry free sleep since we arrived in the country.

Next morning we set out early, determined to catch the first ferry out of Casablanca.

When we arrived at the port we were completely demoralised when we enquired about the next ferry to leave for the Canaries. We were in the tail end of September and were told that the next ferry was not until late December.

At this point, all we wanted to do was to get out of Morocco as soon as possible, but where to go? So we made up our minds to get back to Spain in the shortest amount of time possible.

We were going to drive the 300 and odd miles without stopping, but we had a stroke of luck. If we stuck to our plan, it would mean having to sleep overnight in Tangier, which filled us with dread.

As it was, we stopped to pick up two western looking hitchers; they were a couple of Canadians. We shared our horror stories that we had all encountered in this lawless land. They told us that they were hoping to make it to a hippy commune called 'Hope House,' in the centre of Tangier. They were sure that they would put us up for the night.

When we arrived there, we were welcomed and shown great hospitality. The mixture of races were varied Americans, Canadians, Dutch, English, French and many more.

They were set up to help non-Arab prisoners who were arrested on a daily basis. They would visit each morning and provide a service to the unfortunate inmates by contacting their families back home to inform them that their kin were incarcerated in the hope that maybe they would send money for their fines.

It was so easy to fall foul of the law as it was a simple 'Institutionalised' money making system.

The way it worked was as follows. In Morocco you are pestered non-stop everywhere you go to buy Hashish. Some people would buy the stuff just to stop being harassed. Once you bought any dope, the person who sold it to you would immediately find the nearest policeman who would stop and search you. All the police carried little scales on their belts. They would weigh it, and depending on the amount, would issue the offender with an on the spot fine. If the fine couldn't be paid, then you were arrested and taken straight to jail. If you could pay the fine then the dealer who sold it to you would receive a percentage of the fine and be given back his drugs.

The authorities appreciated the work that 'Hope House' did because it was the money owed for the fines that they were interested in, as keeping people locked up cost them money.

They suggested we try Gibraltar for work instead of Spain. This made a lot of sense, so the next morning we caught the ferry to the Rock, but this was after we gave them a donation as they only survived on charity.

# Chapter 29
## Gibraltar

The next day we drove to the port to take Bessie and us across to the Rock, but when we arrived at customs we were in for a cultural shock. We weren't allowed to enter through customs, as Bessie didn't have Gibraltarian licence plates. Another shock was insurance.

In the '70s, to drive your vehicle on the continent you would need a Green Card to supplement your British insurance, except in Spain where you would need a 'Bail Bond.'

Unfortunately, Gibraltar didn't recognise any of these, and you had to have their own insurance and number plates. They didn't even recognise the UK driving licence.

This was, in part, the ongoing dispute between Britain and Spain over Sovereignty of the Rock, and the land border between them had been closed for many years.

At first I thought they were being prejudiced against 'hippies' and the like, but no, the person in the queue in front of me was the new Navel Surgeon for the Rock, and he received the same treatment as us. Our vehicles were put in a custom shed. They would stay there until the relevant papers were obtained.

Our priority was now to find somewhere to live, and the customs officers suggested a government hostel near the port. We booked in there, then went out looking for work; at least I did.

I found a small English pub frequented by travelling free spirits, such as myself. Angus rarely went out as it would involve spending money. My fortune turned before the first week was out just by using this pub as a base. One night, the elderly landlord informed me that they were looking for crane drivers down at the naval dockyard. He gave me a number to ring, but said not to bother until after the weekend.

This was even better, as my thoughts went to 'Hope House' in Tangier. They always said they would help me at any time, and I did leave them with a generous donation for food. So the next day, I took Bessie back to Morocco and was welcomed warmly at the commune. They said I could leave her there in their compound for as long as I liked, which I did. I insisted that they take a donation from me every two weeks, which they reluctantly agreed to. So every fortnight I would go back briefly, just to take them food and money. Needless to say Angus never went back once we had left.

I went for my interview as a crane driver. I knew I would have to be economical with the truth, but it would have been stupid of me to uphold my lie in case they said, "Here's your crane, let's see what you can do."

I told them that the only cranes I had operated were inside a factory, running back and forth on an overhead rail. I hated lying but it worked. To my surprise, they said they would train me, and give me a test after three weeks. The wages were much worse than I had expected.

I passed the test with flying colours, and after a month I put a word in for Angus, who was hired on the same terms as me. Our main job was assisting on the dry docks, where Navy ships were being repaired or updated, and occasionally we had to put gangplanks onto visiting ships.

At least with a job and money coming in, Angus had stopped moaning and groaning so much.

After we had been working for six months, we were about to have the biggest bust up of our relatively short acquaintance. This really shows what I had to put up with.

Being a betting man, I placed a bet very often, but with low stakes. I hardly ever won because I only backed outsiders. One day, Angus called me a fool for throwing my money away (no argument there). So I challenged him to do better, at no cost to him.

I asked him to pick four horses, and I would put a £1 stake on and we would split the winnings. We won just over ten pounds the first time, and every day for a week, the worst we did was to get our stake money back. He decided that enough was enough, and he wouldn't take part again. I literally begged him to carry on, I pleaded with him and said, "Just wait until we lose, just once," and anyway it was never his stake in the first place. He wouldn't budge, even though we came close to blows. I realised more than ever that I had to end our friendship and go our separate ways.

We made quite a few friends who we mixed with socially, but one in particular, a Geordie from Newcastle, called George. Again, he was similar to Paul, Eugene, and Sandy in character, and like them he came into my life suddenly and departed just as quickly. After saying that, I couldn't be sure that he was a covert investigator.

The fact that I now worked in a sensitive security environment, made it not beyond reason that it was possible. George was a carpenter and on contract to the MOD for a set period.

During the year that I had worked there, I was in constant touch with two past friends, one a girl I had left behind in Jersey, and Don.

Don's romance had blossomed, and they had set a date for their marriage and wanted me to be best man. I hadn't had a holiday in all this time, so I applied for the date of Don's wedding to take a two week vacation. I couldn't believe that they kept turning me down with silly excuses. I pushed and pushed for a reason for not being granted a holiday. So I had to tell Don to look for another 'best man', as I couldn't guarantee being there. Finally the docks administrators gave in, but with the proviso that I would not be given holiday pay when I went. I would be paid when I returned.

I eventually found out why they were so draconian. It was because every time a UK worker took leave, they never returned. The foreman over the cranes spoke up and vouched for me.

This made me angry, as I had now suffered enough of the bureaucracy, and made up my mind to leave, holiday pay or no holiday pay. The money I had saved was intended for my return air fare. This I would use now to drive back in old faithful Bessie.

Of course, I had kept all my plans a secret as far as Angus was concerned. I needed a right time to tell him, but fate intervened.

On the weekend I had planned to tell him, I found my hand was forced by a weird accident.

We were out on the town the Friday night before, and early on that evening, we were walking along the narrow streets going from pub to pub. There were no footpaths and I was walking in front of Angus when I heard a lorry behind us. I looked back to see a Coca Cola lorry approaching. There were many doorways along the street to jump into allowing traffic to pass, as was the norm. I shouted to Angus to get off the street, but belligerent being his middle name, he just squeezed himself up against the wall.

The driver apparently assumed that like all pedestrians, we would take shelter. It may have looked funny, but it wasn't. The side of the lorry rolled Angus along the wall, as if he were a carpet being rolled up, until a gap in a doorway allowed him to be ejected into an entrance way and to safety.

He could hardly breathe as his rib cage must have taken most of the trauma.

The ambulance soon arrived, and he was taken to hospital. I went to see him the next day, and took no pleasure informing him of my immediate plans for departure. He was lucky that the injuries were superficial, except for a couple of cracked ribs. To say that he was angry at my plans would be an understatement. His main complaint was money, and the following day on the Sunday, he had worked out how much I owed him for his share of the petrol in getting down to Gibraltar. He was serious and adamant that I recompense him. I told him he was mad and said goodbye. That was the last time that I saw or heard from him.

If I put off leaving, even for just one day, I might not have made it back to Don's wedding in time.

George surprised me when I told him that I was leaving the next morning. He asked would I mind if he travelled back with me as he wanted to return home.

I was overjoyed at the prospect of not having to travel back alone. I couldn't understand how someone on a government contract could just up and leave without giving notice.

It was with mixed emotions that I left the Rock, and I found that George and I were well suited. I can't remember us having even a small dispute or an argument of any kind during our trip back. After Angus, it felt like I was on a holiday, as we stopped at many varied towns and had some great nights out on our leisurely road trip. It took us just under two weeks to arrive back in England.

The plan was that I would head for London and meet up with Jackie, the last girlfriend that I had when in Jersey. She had now acquired a flat in Wimbledon, but when she greeted me she introduced me to her new boyfriend, which was a bit of a bummer.

I dropped off George at one of the London stations for him to catch a train to Newcastle, but he surprised me by giving me his complete set of carpentry tools, some of which looked brand new, and most seemed that they had hardly been used at all.

He knew that I wasn't broke, and that I had enough money to scrape by on, but insisted that I should take them and sell them if I needed to. That was the last I heard of him.

My very next stop was my old mate Trevor and his wife Brenda, who still lived in Bracknell. They put me up for a couple of nights, and fed and watered me.

Don was to be married in Mansfield in four days' time, which gave me time to stay in my home town of Redditch for a couple of nights. During these two nights, I was out on the town with my mates when a beautiful young girl with frizzy hair and the shortest mini skirt that I had ever seen entered the pub with a group of friends. I had always been sceptical of the phrase 'love at first sight,' but I was stricken. I never had time to speak to her, or even knew her name, but I said to my mates, "See her, that's who I'm going to marry."

I didn't see her again for three months, but a year later she became my wife and life. My itchy feet were cured, but Gail and I had many adventures together in the years to come.